HOME CANNING
AND
PRESERVING

HOME CANNING AND PRESERVING

Joan and Monte Burch

Reston Publishing Company, Inc.
Reston, Virginia
A Prentice-Hall Company

Library of Congress Cataloging in Publication Data

Burch, Joan.
    Home canning and preserving.

    Includes index.
    1. Canning and preserving.   I.   Burch, Monte, joint
author.   II. Title.
TX603.B897   641.4   76–41881
ISBN 0-87909-351-X

©1977 by
Reston Publishing Company, Inc.
A Prentice-Hall Company
Reston, Virginia 22090

10   9   8   7   6   5   4   3   2   1

Printed in the United States of America.

CONTENTS

PREFACE

Why put up your own food when you can easily buy what you need at the supermarket? There are many reasons, but probably the most important one is economy. You can put up fresh fruits and vegetables and make jams, jellies, and pickles for a fraction of the cost of the same items at the grocery store. And, if you're lucky enough to have a bountiful garden, you'll really be able to save on your food bill. Other good reasons for preserving food are the pleasure of producing something and the feeling of independence. In these modern times when millions of lives depend on the food-producing ability of a comparative handful, being able to produce and preserve your own food is not only a source of pride, pleasure and independence, but possibly a lifesaver as well.

In the past few years, a great demand for canning and freezing supplies has developed which manufacturers have not always been able to meet. One reason for this demand is that the rush to our urban areas is over; more and more people are returning to a rural life and the independence of growing and preserving their own food. Unfortunately, much of the information our grandfathers and grandmothers passed down from generation to generation has been lost in the mad rush to the city.

Today, much of the all-important technology of food preservation is still to be learned.

One facet of rural life that *has* been preserved in the Burch family and handed down from generation to generation is how to grow, preserve, store, and prepare our own food. We learned directly from our grand-parents and parents how to slaughter pork, salt and cure it for storage; how to grow a garden and orchard, and how to preserve the bounty. For several years we have lived on a farm and have been relearning some of the older, as well as the newer, practices of food preservation. Our only hope is that what we have learned can be passed on to the next genera-tion providing them with similar feelings of pride, independence, and pioneer spirit.

We wish to thank all of the good people who have contributed their knowledge, time, photographs, and charts for this book, including the U.S. Department of Agriculture.

JOAN BURCH
MONTE BURCH

HOME CANNING
AND
PRESERVING

1

CANNING FRUITS,
VEGETABLES,
AND MEATS

THE BASICS OF CANNING

For many years man lived from day to day; a hunter and forager. He killed and gathered what food he could eat before it spoiled. Gradually man learned to cultivate certain foods so he would have a more adequate supply. He also learned to dry, smoke, and salt meats, and fruits and vegetables to carry him through the times of no game and the seasons when plants didn't produce. These age-old methods of food preservation were the only methods for centuries. Today, smoked and dried meats and fruits are considered a delicacy, but they weren't much more than hard, tasteless foods in earlier times. In 1809, Nicholas Appert, a French chef, discovered that foods could be preserved indefinitely if they were placed in glass containers—the containers sealed, then boiled. He discovered that it required a different amount of time to preserve fruits, vegetables, jellies, and syrups. His containers were glass bottles sealed with cork "lids," held in place by wire and sealing wax. As a result of his discovery, he became known as the "father of canning."

Today's canning methods and equipment are more advanced than those of the early days; however, they are still the same basic methods and one of the best ways to home preserve food. Home canning is economical, self-satisfying, and a good way of gaining a bit of independence, but you must adhere to the safety rules of canning. To understand the methods of canning, you must understand the reasons for food spoilage.

FOOD SPOILAGE

There are basically three different microorganisms that can cause spoilage of food: molds, yeasts, and bacteria. Molds are fuzzy patches found on the tops of improperly sealed jelly glasses; yeasts are the cause of food fermenting; and bacteria cause food to become flat-sour, soft, and slimy. These tiny microorganisms are everywhere—in the air, water, and the soil. All of these spoilage microorganisms are affected by the amount of salt, sugar, and moisture in the produce. They all require moisture to grow, and when there is no moisture, they won't grow. However, as soon as moisture and favorable conditions are applied, the seeds or spores of the microorganisms will start growing again.

One of the earliest methods of food preservation was a brine solution of salt and water. These brine solutions are designated 5%, 10%, and 15% according to the amount of salt. Some organisms are stopped by a 5% brine solution, while others require a 15% solution. Sugar also helps prevent the growth of particular bacteria, usually at a concentration of 50% to 60%. At 70%, almost all bacteria growth is halted.

Another important factor in proper food preservation is the acid-strength of the food. Plants with more acid strength require less time or lower temperatures in order to destroy the spoilage molds, yeasts, or bacteria. Because of modern findings relating to acid strength, time, and temperature, it is no longer recommended that water bath canning be used for low-acid foods. Some bacteria are quite hardy, and a high heat is required to kill them.

The worst danger in canning (not only home canning but occasionally commercial canning) is the development of bacillus botulism, a poisonous toxin produced by certain bacteria growing in certain canned food. Botulism toxin is one of the most powerful poisons known to man and can result in death if not treated quickly and properly.

There are several rules that must be strictly adhered to in order to insure against botulism poisoning:

1. Make sure all processing equipment is clean and in good shape.
2. Make sure the pressure gauge on the pressure canner is accurate.
3. Follow carefully the processing times recommended by your canner manufacturer.
4. Since the toxin can be destroyed by boiling, it is recommended that you boil all low-acid, home-canned foods before serving *or tasting*. They should be boiled 10 minutes. Spinach, greens, corn, and meat should be boiled 15 minutes.
5. Don't take any shortcuts in canning. Follow only reliable, up-to-date methods.
6. All nonacid foods and meats should be processed in a pressure canner only.

Most molds and yeasts are found on fruits and tomatoes because the foods are higher in acid content. They are destroyed when the food is processed in a boiling water bath at 212°F. Bacteria, however, are found in low-acid foods such as green beans. Because bacteria are harder to destroy, low-acid foods should be processed at 240°F in a pressure steam canner. The acidity of the food, the temperature and time under which it is processed, how many microorganisms are present in the food, and how fast the heat penetrates to the center of the canning jar, are all important in food canning.

EQUIPMENT NEEDED

For water bath canning, you'll need either a large metal container or a regular canner. The container must be from 3 to 5 inches deeper than the canning jars as shown below. A canner should also have a good, proper-fitting cover and a wire rack for lifting jars out and for keeping them from touching or falling against the sides of the canner during processing. A steam pressure canner can be used for the water bath canning if it is deep enough.

For pressure canning, you'll need a regulation steam-pressure canner which may be purchased at mail-order stores, hardware stores, etc. It has a cover that may be clamped down tightly, a safety valve, a vent, and a pressure gauge of some sort. Newer canners often use a combination weighted-vent gauge control that "whistles" to indicate the pressure. The dial pressure gauge should be tested at least once a year for accuracy. Check with your local county agent about where it should be tested.

Naturally, you will also need canning jars. These may be reused indefinitely as long as they're well taken care of and aren't cracked or chipped. In the water bath method, you can use jars that are sized to hold rings and lids, such as mayonnaise jars. When pressure canning,

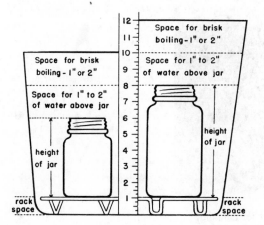

however, use only jars made especially for home canning. Lids may be either dome caps with rings or zinc caps with rubber rings. Although metal cans have been used in the past for home canning, they are hard to get, and we don't suggest their use anymore. They are another part of the throw-away, disposable society we need to give up.

In addition to these main items, you'll need several small items: a jar lifter, tongs, a jar funnel, measuring spoons, large containers for preparing hot packed foods, washing containers, paring knives, a table knife to remove air bubbles from jars, large spoons, and a timer or clock.

GENERAL CANNING METHODS

Canning is not one of those last-minute, rush-into things; it should be well planned out. Make sure you understand the instructions and have the proper equipment on hand as well as the produce you intend to can. It's a good idea to plan your garden so you have a successive ripening of produce. It's much easier to can a few items every morning rather than spending a couple of full days canning a huge batch of produce that is ripening too quickly. It's also a good idea to can small amounts of a variety of foods rather than one large batch that your family will quickly tire of. Make sure you have plenty of jars and lids on hand; this often means purchasing materials out of season, because during the canning season, your local dealer may quickly run out. Pints are normally the most convenient jars if you're canning for two or three persons, and they are also best for such items as pickles, jams, and jellies. The day before you plan to can, go through your assortment of jars,

Some of the equipment needed for canning.

rings, etc., and check the jars for any nicks or chips that might prevent them from sealing properly. Check the rings to make sure that they aren't rusted or out of shape. Discard any items that are unsuitable for reuse. It's a good idea at this time to thoroughly wash all metal rings or zinc caps and jars in hot soapy water and then rinse in clean, running hot water. Jars shouldn't be washed with steel brushes or other metal objects, as you may damage the glass. Prepare metal lids or "flats" and/or rubber rings according to the manufacturer's directions.

The morning that you plan to can, gather all equipment and make sure you have everything you need. Pick fresh, firm ripe fruits or vegetables; then wash thoroughly in small lots, changing water several times or using running water. It's a good idea to wash only as much as you can prepare in one canner load at a time. Handle gently, and try to keep from bruising the produce. Make sure you have all dirt off to eliminate as much bacteria as possible.

If you have to harvest or purchase produce but can't prepare it quickly, place it in a cool, dry, airy place. Above all, don't try to can poor produce—canning won't help improve the flavor or goodness in bad produce; it will only make it worse. Any vegetables that are wilted or tough will taste just the same. Spoiled or bruised fruits will also taste the same.

PACKING

There are two methods of packing food into jars: *hot pack* and *raw pack*. In the raw pack method, the food is unheated, simply packed raw into the jars, and then covered with a boiling hot liquid. In the hot pack method, food is preheated in liquid, packed hot into jars, and then covered with the hot cooking liquid.

In most cases, raw packed fruits and vegetables should be packed fairly tight into the glass jars, as they will shrink when processed. However, some foods such as peas, lima beans, and corn will expand when processed, so they should be packed loosely. Hot packed foods are usually packed fairly loose. It's a good idea to run a kitchen knife blade down inside the jar in several places. This will force out the air bubbles and distribute the food more evenly in the jar. If the food is not covered with liquid, add enough syrup, juice, or water to completely fill in around and cover the solid food in the container. If the food isn't covered completely, the food on top will darken; however, this will not affect the taste of the food.

The jars shouldn't be completely filled. There should be a certain amount of air space between the food and the top of the jar. This not only allows the jar to seal more properly, but allows for the expansion of food as it is heated. The amount of head space varies with different foods, so follow directions for each particular type of food.

CLOSING JARS

After properly filling, wipe around the sealing edge of the jar to insure that no food hampers the seal. There are three basic methods of closing jars:

Metal Screwband and Flat. These are equipped with a sealing compound. In this method, after wiping the rim clean, place the flat or lid in place on the jar; then screw the metal screwband down over the flat. The metal band should only be turned down handtight and should not be tightened further after removing from the canner. As soon as the jars are cool from the processing, you can remove the screw rings and save them for reuse. However, metal flats cannot be reused except for freezing. If you can't get a band to come off easily, cover it with a hot damp cloth for a moment.

Porcelain-Lined Zinc Caps. These reusable lids require a rubber shoulder ring for the seal. The washed and wet rubber rings are first fitted down over the jar top and down against the sealing shoulder. Don't stretch the rubber ring more than necessary. The jars are then filled and the top rim and rubber ring wiped clean. The zinc caps are turned down tightly against the rubber ring and then turned back 1/4 turn. When you

Metal screw cap

Metal lid with sealing compound

Seals here

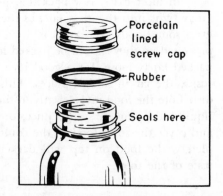

Porcelain lined screw cap

Rubber

Seals here

remove the jars from the canner, turn the screw cap back down tightly to complete the seal. You can reuse good zinc caps but not the rubber rings. To remove the zinc caps easily, pull out the tab on the rubber ring with a pair of pliers. This loosens the seal and lets the cap come off easily without ruining the cap.

Glass Tops With Bails. These also require the use of new rubber rings. After filling jars, wipe top clean, and add glass top. Place the long wire in the groove and leave the short wire up. After processing, complete seal by pressing down short wire.

PROCESSING

After filling and closing the jars, they are processed, again using a boiling-water bath canner for pickles, tomatoes, and fruits, and a steam pressure canner for all low-acid vegetables and meats. Make sure you have read your time chart for the proper amount of processing time, and follow rules carefully for the kind of food and canner you're using.

COOLING CANNED FOOD

After the food has been processed, it must be handled carefully. The jars are extremely hot and need to be cooled gradually. Carefully remove the jars from the canner using a jar lifter. Set on a rack or a folded cloth, and complete the seals if necessary. If a portion of the liquid has boiled out during processing, leave the jar as is; don't attempt to open the jar and add more, as this will only break the seal. Set the jars upright in a good safe place out of a draft. Don't set them on a cold surface, and don't attempt to slow down the cooling by covering with a cloth.

TESTING JAR SEALS

As soon as the jars have cooled properly, normally 12 to 24 hours, test to make sure they have sealed. On the screw ring and flat caps, push down on the center of the cap. If it is already down and will not move up or down, the jar is properly sealed. If it moves up and down, it isn't sealed. You can also test by tapping on the jar lid with a spoon. If there is a clear ringing sound, the jar is sealed. However, if the sound is dull, the jar may not necessarily be unsealed; look for signs of leakage. If sealed, remove the screwband, wipe jar clean with a soft cloth, and store in a cool, dark, dry storage area. It's also helpful to label and date your products.

To test zinc caps and glass lids for sealing, check for leakage. If the jars do not leak, they are sealed.

If you discover any unsealed jars, you can recan them as before. But if they won't seal as sometimes happens, or if you prefer, you can place them in the refrigerator and use immediately.

STORING CANNED FOODS

Storage for canned foods can be anything from a basement to a garage; however, it should not be damp, and the jars should not be allowed to freeze. If the room is too damp, the metal lids will rust. Also if the room is too warm, it may cause the food to lose taste or change color, as will storing in a bright sunny room. If food has to be stored in an unheated room that might freeze, wrap the jars in blankets or cover them in some way. If the canned food does freeze, it is not necessarily ruined. Freezing does not affect the food but can break the jar or break the seal and cause the food to spoil. Occasionally examine stored canned foods for spoilage. A leak around a jar lid or a bulging lid means spoiled food.

Examine every jar you open carefully for any signs of spoilage, such as bulging lids or leakage. If there is an odor, mold, or spurting liquid when jar is opened, discard the food by burning so it cannot possibly be eaten by humans or animals.

Again, the food may contain botulism bacteria and may not show any sign of spoilage, so heat all vegetables to a rolling boil, then cover and boil them for at least 10 minutes. Spinach, other greens, corn, and meat should be boiled for at least 20 minutes. At high altitudes, boil at least 5 minutes longer. If at anytime during heating the food appears spoiled, has an odor, or foams, destroy it. Boiling the food for the lengths of time mentioned will kill any botulism bacteria.

CANNING FRUITS AND
HIGH-ACID VEGETABLES

Fruits and high-acid vegetables such as tomatoes, sauerkraut, and rhubarb are canned in a water bath canner using either raw or hot pack.

In raw pack, the cold raw fruits are packed into the containers, and boiling-hot juice, syrup, or water is poured in to cover them. When doing tomatoes in this manner, they are pressed down into the containers until they are covered by their own juice; no other liquid is added. In hot pack, the foods are heated in water, syrup, steam, or extracted juice, and packed and covered with the hot liquid.

Sugar is used in canning fruits to help them hold their shape, color, and flavor. In most cases, this sweetening is used as a syrup. To make up the syrup, stir the sugar in with water or juice, boil 5 minutes, and skim off any foam.

There are three different types of syrup which may be used, depending on your taste and the sweetness of the fruit:

4 cups of water	2 cups sugar	For 5 cups THIN syrup.
or juice	3 cups sugar	For 5½ cups MEDIUM syrup.
	4¾ cups sugar	For 6½ cups HEAVY syrup.

If juicy fruit is to be packed hot, you can add ½ cup sugar to each quart of the raw prepared fruit. Then heat to simmering and pack the fruit in the juice that has cooked out.

Light corn syrup or mild-flavored honey can be used to replace half of the sugar; however, don't use brown sugar, sorghum, or molasses, as the flavor and color may change the fruit.

You can, however, can fruit without adding this additional sweetening by canning the fruit in its own extracted juice or in water. The processing time is the same as for sweetened fruit. The sugar does not help prevent spoilage.

WATER BATH PROCESSING

Place the packed jars into a water bath canner about half-filled with water. If raw packing, the water in the canner should be hot but not boiling. For hot packed fruits and vegetables, use boiling water. Lower the jars into the canner, and pour in more boiling or hot water to bring the water level up over the tops of the jars by an inch or two. However, make sure you don't pour boiling water directly on the jars. Place the canner cover in place.

As soon as the water in the canner comes to a rolling boil, start counting the processing time. Keep the water boiling gently and steadily for the time recommended for the particular food you are processing. The times given for individual foods in this book should be adjusted according to your altitude as shown. If at any time the water level drops below the tops of the jars, add more boiling water.

Altitude	Increase in processing time if the time called for is—	
	20 minutes or less	More than 20 minutes
1,000 feet	1 minute	2 minutes.
2,000 feet	2 minutes	4 minutes.
3,000 feet	3 minutes	6 minutes.
4,000 feet	4 minutes	8 minutes.
5,000 feet	5 minutes	10 minutes.
6,000 feet	6 minutes	12 minutes.
7,000 feet	7 minutes	14 minutes.
8,000 feet	8 minutes	16 minutes.
9,000 feet	9 minutes	18 minutes.
10,000 feet	10 minutes	20 minutes.

After food has processed for the correct amount of time, turn off the heat, allow the water to cool somewhat, remove canner lid, and using jar tongs, remove jars from canner and handle as mentioned earlier.

You may be interested in the following chart, which gives approximate amounts of canned fruit you can expect from fresh fruits. However, remember that the quality, size, variety, and maturity of the fruits will also have a great deal of effect. But in general, the following amounts of fruits will make up one quart of canned food.

Fruit	Pounds
Apples	2½ to 3
Berries, except strawberries	1½ to 3 (1 to 2 quart boxes)
Cherries (canned unpitted)	2 to 2½
Peaches	2 to 3
Pears	2 to 3
Plums	1½ to 2½
Tomatoes	2½ to 3½

DIRECTIONS FOR CANNING FRUITS AND TOMATOES

Apples

Wash, peel, and core apples. Slice, cut into chunks, or leave in quarters. As you prepare apples, drop them in a solution of 1 tablespoon each salt and vinegar to 2 quarts of water to prevent darkening. Drain well, rinse, and drain again.

Hot Pack Only—Boil apples 5 minutes in syrup or water, and pack hot into clean, hot jars. Cover with the boiling liquid and leave ½ inch headspace. Process in boiling water bath:

Pint Jars	15 minutes
Quart Jars	20 minutes

Remove from canner, and complete seals if necessary.

Applesauce

Prepare applesauce and sweeten if desired. Ascorbic acid may be added to prevent darkening, ½ teaspoon per quart of fruit.

Hot Pack Only—Heat applesauce to between 185°F and 210°F, stirring often to keep from sticking, and pack hot into clean, hot jars leaving ¼ inch headspace. Process in boiling water bath:

Pint Jars	10 minutes
Quart Jars	10 minutes

Remove from canner, and complete seals if necessary.

Apricots

Apricots may be canned, peeled, unpeeled, left whole, in pitted halves, or sliced. To slip peels, dip in boiling water for 1 minute, and cool quickly in cold water.

Raw Pack—Pack into hot jars and cover with a boiling syrup leaving ½ inch headspace. Process in boiling water bath:

Pint Jars	25 minutes
Quart Jars	30 minutes

Hot Pack—Prepare as directed above and boil 1 to 3 minutes in syrup; then pack into hot clean jars to ½ inch from top, and process in boiling water bath:

Pint Jars   20 minutes

Quart Jars   25 minutes

Remove from canner, and complete seals if necessary.

Berries, Firm (Blueberries, Currants, Elderberries, Huckleberries, and Gooseberries)

Wash and drain, remove stems, etc. Add ½ cup sugar to each quart of berries.

Hot Pack Only—Heat berries and sugar to boiling, stirring and shaking pan often to keep from sticking, pack hot into clean, hot jars to within ½ inch from top, and process in boiling water bath:

Pint Jars   10 minutes

Quart Jars   15 minutes

Remove from canner, and complete seals if necessary.

Berries, Soft (Blackberries, Dewberries, Loganberries, Raspberries, except Strawberries)

Wash and drain berries, and remove stems, etc.

Raw Pack Only—Fill clean hot jars with berries, and cover with boiling syrup to within ½ inch from top. Process in boiling water bath:

Pint Jars   10 minutes

Quart Jars   15 minutes

Remove from canner, and complete seals if necessary.

Cherries

Wash cherries, and remove stems and pits.

Raw Pack— Fill clean, hot jars with cherries, and cover with a boiling syrup to within ½ inch from top. Process in boiling water bath:

Pint Jars   20 minutes

Quart Jars   25 minutes

Hot Pack—Add ½ cup sugar to each quart of pitted cherries, and bring to a boil. Pack into hot, clean jars to within ½ inch from top, and process in boiling water bath:

Pint Jars	10 minutes
Quart Jars	15 minutes

Remove jars from canner, and complete seals if necessary.

Fruit Purees

Prepare, pack, and process as for applesauce, adding sugar if desired.

Grapefruit

Wash and peel grapefruit, remove each segment from the white membrane, and discard all seeds.

Raw Pack Only—Pack segments into clean, hot jars, and cover with a very light syrup or juice heated to simmering (185°F to 210°F). Leave 1 to 1½ inches of headspace. Process in a simmering water bath (185°F to 210°F):

Pint Jars	30 minutes
Quart Jars	35 minutes

Remove jars from canner, and complete seals if necessary.

Peaches

Wash and peel peaches. To slip skins, dip peaches in boiling water for a few seconds and then into cold water. Peaches can be prepared in slices, quarters, or halves. Smaller peaches may be left whole. To prevent darkening, place prepared peaches in a solution of 1 tablespoon each salt and vinegar to 2 quarts of water. Drain well before packing.

Raw Pack—Prepare peaches, and pack into jars. Cover with boiling syrup to within ½ inch from top, and process in boiling water bath:

Pint Jars	25 minutes
Quart Jars	30 minutes

Left, to peel peaches, scald in boiling water, then cool in cold water. *Right*, hot packed peaches are first heated in syrup, then packed into jars. *Above*, boiling syrup is added to cover the peaches.

Hot Pack—Prepare peaches, and bring to boiling in syrup until peaches are heated throughout. Pack into clean, hot jars to within ½ inch from top, and cover with syrup. Process in boiling water bath:

Pint Jars   20 minutes

Quart Jars   25 minutes

Pears

Wash, peel, cut in half, and core pears. Leave in halves, or cut into quarters. Prepare as peaches using either hot or cold pack. Use the cold pack only for pears that are juicy ripe.

Pineapple

Peel, remove eyes, and core. Leave pineapple in slices, cut in chunks, or crush.

Hot Pack Only—Boil pineapple in a light syrup or unsweetened juice until heated through; then pack into clean, hot jars. Leave $\frac{1}{2}$ inch headspace and process in boiling water bath:

Pint Jars	20 minutes
Quart Jars	20 minutes

Remove jars from canner, and complete seals if necessary.

Plums

Wash plums, and prick skins with a needle if you wish to can them whole. Freestone plums can be cut in half and pitted.

Raw Pack—Prepare fruit, and pack into clean, hot jars. Cover with a boiling syrup to within $\frac{1}{2}$ inch from top, and process in boiling water bath:

Pint Jars	20 minutes
Quart Jars	25 minutes

Hot Pack—Prepare fruit, heat to boiling in syrup, and pack hot into clean, hot jars. Cover with syrup to within $\frac{1}{2}$ inch from top, and process in boiling water bath:

Pint Jars	20 minutes
Quart Jars	25 minutes

Remove jars from canner, and complete seals if necessary.

Rhubarb

Wash and cut into $\frac{1}{2}$ inch pieces.

Raw Pack—Prepare rhubarb, pack tightly into jars leaving 1 inch head-space, and cover with boiling syrup. Process in boiling water bath:

Pint Jars	10 minutes
Quart Jars	10 minutes

Hot Pack—Prepare rhubarb, and add ½ cup sugar to each quart of fruit. Let stand until juicy; then heat to boiling. Pack hot into clean, hot jars leaving ½ inch headspace. Process in boiling water bath:

Pint Jars	10 minutes
Quart Jars	10 minutes

Remove jars from canner, and complete seals if necessary.

Strawberries

These are best frozen. If this is not possible, dry them, or make jams, jellies, or preserves from the crop.

Tomatoes

Wash tomatoes, slip skins by dipping into boiling water and then into cold water. Peel and remove stem ends. Tomatoes can be prepared whole, in halves, or in quarters.

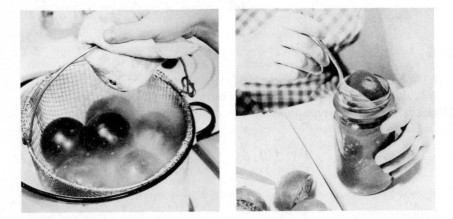

Left, to peel tomatoes, first scald in boiling water, then cool in cold water. *Right,* for raw packed tomatoes, pack the jars with the peeled tomatoes pressing until juice covers the tomatoes; no other liquid is added.

Raw Pack— Pack prepared tomatoes into jars leaving ½ inch headspace. Pack tightly, and press until juice covers tomatoes. Do not add water. Add ½ teaspoon salt to each pint and 1 teaspoon to each quart. Process in boiling water bath:

Pint Jars	35 minutes
Quart Jars	45 minutes

Hot Pack—Prepare tomatoes and heat to boiling in their own juice. Pack into clean hot jars, leaving ½ inch headspace. Add salt as above and process in boiling water bath:

Pint Jars	10 minutes
Quart Jars	10 minutes

Remove jars from canner, and complete seals if necessary.

LOW-ACID VEGETABLES

All low-acid vegetables should be processed in a steam-pressure canner, following the directions of your particular canner manufacturer. Again, these can be either raw packed or hot packed. Vegetables except corn, peas, and lima beans may be packed tightly into the jars and then covered with boiling water. In hot packing, the vegetables are preheated in steam or water and then covered with the cooking liquid or water. The liquid used to cook the vegetables is recommended because it contains many nutrients which would otherwise be lost. However, if the cooking liquid is dark, gritty, or strong flavored, water may be used.

After packing jars as recommended and fastening lids in place, pour 2 to 3 inches of boiling water into the steam canner, or use the amount of water suggested by your canner manufacturer. Place the jars on the rack in the canner, making sure the steam can circulate around each jar. If you place 2 layers of jars in the canner, make sure you use another rack, and stagger the jars so steam can reach all portions of the jars.

Place canner lid in position, and fasten securely according to manufacturer's instructions. Turn on heat, and watch until steam starts to come steadily from the vent. Allow it to steam for 10 minutes to allow all air to escape from the canner, and close petcock or place weighted gauge in place.

Allow the pressure to rise to 10 pounds (240°F); then immediately start counting the processing time. Maintain this pressure constantly by turing up or down the heat under the canner. *Do not by any means use the petcock to lower pressure.* Keep cold, drafty air from blowing on the canner. If using a weighted gauge, you will have to wait until the gauge jiggles; then turn the heat up or down until it jiggles from 1 to 3 times per minute, or according to your manufacturer's instructions. Process according to the time given for each particular food. When processing time is up, remove canner from heat immediately.

Allow the canner to set until the pressure is zero. Don't hurry the cooling by pouring cold water over the canner. When the pressure registers zero, or the weighted gauge won't allow any more steam to escape, slowly open the petcock or remove the weighted gauge with a fork. Carefully unfasten cover, and remove it with one side tilted away from you so there won't be any danger of steam coming into your face. Remove the cover, and using jar tongs, remove the jars, and set them in a safe place out of drafts on a wooden rack or folded cloth.

To pressure can at altitudes above sea level, you will need to process the food at higher pressures. Add 1 pound of pressure for each 2000 feet above sea level. At 2000 feet above sea level, 10 pounds of pressure would become 11 pounds. Weighted gauges used at high altitude canning will have to be corrected by the manufacturer, or follow high-altitude instructions in your pressure canner book.

Dial gauges should be checked at least once each year to see if they are registering the correct amount of pressure. Check with your local county extension office or dealer for information about getting your gauge checked. If the gauge is off less than 5 pounds, use the following chart to compensate. However, if the gauge is more than 5 pounds off, you should get a new gauge. These figures are for a normal processing at 10 pounds pressure:

If the gauge reads high—	*If the gauge reads low—*
1 pound high—process at 11 pounds.	1 pound low—process at 9 pounds.
2 pounds high—process at 12 pounds.	2 pounds low—process at 8 pounds.
3 pounds high—process at 13 pounds.	3 pounds low—process at 7 pounds.
4 pounds high—process at 14 pounds.	4 pounds low—process at 6 pounds.

If you use a pressure saucepan for canning, add 20 minutes to the processing time of all vegetables and meats to allow for the rapid heating and cooling of the smaller pan.

You can figure the amount of vegetables that will be canned according to the following chart. The amount of vegetables normally needed for one quart of canned food are as follows:

	Pounds		*Pounds*
Asparagus	2½ to 4½	Okra	1½
Beans, lima, in pods	3 to 5	Peas, green, in pods	3 to 6
Beans, snap	1½ to 2½	Pumpkin or winter squash	1½ to 3
Beets, without tops	2 to 3½	Spinach and other greens	2 to 6
Carrots, without tops	2 to 3	Squash, summer	2 to 4
Corn, sweet, in husks	3 to 6	Sweet potatoes	2 to 3

When canning vegetables, salt is added at the rate of ½ teaspoon per pint and 1 teaspoon per quart. Always use canning or pickling salt. Add the salt to each jar after they are filled. Vegetables can also be canned salt-free. A sugar-salt mixture can be added to such vegetables as peas and corn. Mix 2 parts sugar with 1 part salt, and add 1 teaspoon of this mixture to each pint of vegetables in place of the salt. Be sure to label your jars of vegetables exactly, so you will later know how to serve them.

DIRECTIONS FOR CANNING LOW-ACID VEGETABLES

Asparagus

Wash, trim, and cut into 1-inch pieces, or cut into spears approximately 1 inch shorter than your widemouth jars.

Raw Pack—Pack into jars, add salt, and cover with boiling water to within ½ inch from top. Process at 10 pounds pressure:

> Pint and Half-Pint Jars   25 minutes
> Quart Jars   30 minutes

Hot Pack—Cover prepared asparagus with boiling water, and cook about 2 minutes. Pack hot, and cover with boiling liquid to with ½ inch from top. Add salt, and process at 10 pounds pressure:

> Pint and Half-Pint Jars   25 minutes
> Quart Jars   30 minutes

Remove jars from canner, and complete seals if necessary.

Beans, Baked

Cover dried beans with boiling water, and bring to boiling again. Remove from heat, and let soak for 1 hour. Drain beans, and prepare as for baked beans in your oven or in a slow cooker. Bake 4 to 5 hours or until tender. Check often, and add more liquid as needed.

Hot Pack—Pack hot into jars, leaving 1 inch headspace. Process at 10 pounds pressure:

Pint and Half-Pint Jars	80 minutes
Quart Jars	100 minutes

Remove jars from canner, and complete seals if necessary.

Beans, with Pork and Tomato Sauce

Cover dried beans with boiling water, and bring to boiling again. Remove from heat, and let soak for 1 hour. Reheat to boiling, and drain beans. Pack hot beans into jars filling only ¾ full. Add a small piece of salt pork, bacon, or ham to each jar, and cover with boiling tomato sauce to within 1 inch from top. Process at 10 pounds pressure:

Pint and Half-Pint Jars	65 minutes
Quart Jars	75 minutes

Beans, Lima

Shell and wash young, tender limas.

Raw Pack—Pack into jars loosely, leaving 1 inch headspace for pint jars and 1½ inches for quarts. Do not press or shake beans down into jars. Add salt, and fill to within ½ inch with boiling water. Process at 10 pounds:

Pint and Half-Pint Jars	40 minutes
Quart Jars	50 minutes

Hot Pack—Cover shelled beans with boiling water and bring to a boil again. Pack into jars loosely to within 1 inch from top, and cover with boiling liquid. Add salt, and process at 10 pounds pressure for the same time as for raw pack. Remove jars from canner, and complete seals if necessary.

Beans (Snap, String, Wax)

Wash beans and snap, removing ends and breaking into 1 inch pieces. Or leave beans whole, and pack standing up in jars.

Raw Pack—Pack tightly to within ½ inch from top, and cover with boiling water. Add salt, and process at 10 pounds pressure:

| Pint and Half-Pint Jars | 20 minutes |
| Quart Jars | 25 minutes |

Hot Pack—Cover prepared beans with boiling water, and cook 5 minutes. Pack into jars to within ½ inch from top. Add salt, and cover with boiling liquid. Process at 10 pounds pressure for the same time as for raw pack. Remove jars from canner and complete seals if necessary.

Left, to hot pack beans, cover prepared beans with boiling water and cook 5 minutes. *Right,* pack hot beans in jars and cover with boiling cooking liquid.

Beans, Soy

Prepare green soy beans as for lima beans, and process at 10 pounds pressure:

Pint and Half-Pint Jars	55 minutes
Quart Jars	65 minutes

Beets

Wash beets, and remove excess tops leaving about 1 inch. Cover with boiling water, and boil until tender or skins slip easily. Or cook under 15 pounds pressure for 6 minutes. Cool beets in cold water, and remove skins and tops. Sort beets, and prepare according to size. Smaller beets are left whole, larger ones cut in halves or quarters, sliced, or diced. Pack into jars leaving ½ inch headspace, add salt, and cover with boiling water. Process at 10 pounds pressure:

Pint and Half-Pint Jars	30 minutes
Quart Jars	35 minutes

Carrots

Wash and scrape carrots; slice, dice, leave small ones whole, or cut into spears.

Raw Pack—Pack into jars to within 1 inch from top. Add salt, and cover with boiling water to within ½ inch from top. Process at 10 pounds pressure:

Pint and Half-Pint Jars	25 minutes
Quart Jars	30 minutes

Hot Pack—Prepare carrots, and cover with boiling water. Bring back to boil, and pack hot to within ½ inch from top. Add salt, and cover with boiling liquid. Process at 10 pounds pressure for the same time as for raw pack. Remove jars from canner, and complete seals if necessary.

Corn, Cream Style

Remove husks and silks from corn, and wash. Cut from cob and scrape cob. Prepare in pint jars only.

Raw Pack—Pack corn into jars to within 1½ inches from top. Do not pack tightly. Add salt, and fill to within ½ inch from top with boiling water. Process at 10 pounds pressure:

Pint and Half-Pint Jars	95 minutes

Hot Pack—Prepare corn, and measure. Add half as much boiling water as corn, and reheat to boiling. Pack into jars to within 1 inch from top; add salt. Process at 10 pounds pressure:

Pint and Half-Pint Jars	85 minutes

Remove jars from canner, and complete seals if necessary.

Corn, Whole Kernel

Remove husks and silks from corn, and wash. Cut kernels from cobs; do not scrape and do not cut into the cob.

Raw Pack—Pack cut kernels in jars to within 1 inch from top. Do not pack tightly. Add salt, and fill to within ½ inch from top with boiling water. Process at 10 pounds pressure:

Pint and Half-Pint Jars	55 minutes
Quart Jars	85 minutes

Hot Pack—Measure prepared corn, and add half as much boiling water. Reheat to boiling and pack to within 1 inch from top of jars. Add salt, and cover with boiling liquid. Process at 10 pounds pressure for the same time as for raw pack. Remove jars from canner, and complete seals if necessary.

Greens

Prepare only young, tender greens either wild or the garden varieties. Remove tough stems, and wash thoroughly. Boil in small amount of water, turning and stirring constantly until all greens are wilted and have changed color. Pack hot into jars, add salt, and cover with boiling water to within ½ inch from top. Process at 10 pounds pressure:

Pint and Half-Pint Jars	70 minutes
Quart Jars	90 minutes

Hominy

For each quart of shelled dry white or yellow field corn, make a solution of 1 gallon water and 1 ounce lye in an enameled pan. Boil corn in solution until hulls come loose or about 30 minutes. Remove from heat, and let stand another half hour. Drain corn, and rinse several times in hot water; then cool corn by rinsing several more times in cold water. Work kernels with your hands until the dark tips are removed. Cover kernels with water, and rinse until tips are removed. They should float to the top of the water. Cover hominy with water, and boil 5 minutes. Drain and repeat 4 more times; then simmer hominy until tender. One quart of dried corn yields about 3 quarts of hominy.

Hot Pack Only—Pack hot, cooked hominy into jars leaving ½ inch headspace. Add salt, and cover with boiling water. Process at 10 pounds pressure:

<blockquote>

Pint and Half-Pint Jars	60 minutes
Quart Jars	70 minutes

</blockquote>

Remove jars from canner, and complete seals if necessary.

Mushrooms

Trim stems, and soak in cold water to remove all soil. Drain and rinse again. Leave small button mushrooms whole. Halve or quarter larger ones. Heat gently in a covered saucepan for 15 minutes without adding any liquid. Pack hot mushrooms into jars to within ½ inch from top. Add salt (¼ teaspoon for half-pints) and crystalline ascorbic acid (1/16 teaspoon for half-pints and ⅛ teaspoon for pints). Cover with boiling water, and process at 10 pounds pressure:

<blockquote>

Pint and Half-Pint Jars	30 minutes

</blockquote>

Remove jars from canner, and complete seals if necessary.

Okra

Prepare only tender, young pods. Wash and trim; then boil 1 minute. Leave small pods whole; cut others in 1 inch lengths.

Hot Pack Only—Pack hot okra into jars leaving ½ inch headspace. Add salt, and cover with boiling water. Process at 10 pounds pressure:

Pint and Half-Pint Jars	25 minutes
Quart Jars	40 minutes

Peas, Fresh Blackeye, Cowpeas, and Blackeye Beans

Prepare only tender young peas. Shell and wash.

Raw Pack—Pack prepared peas into jars to within 1½ inches from top for pints and 2 inches for quarts. Do not pack tightly. Add salt and cover with boiling water to within ½ inch of top. Process at 10 pounds pressure:

Pint and Half-Pint Jars	35 minutes
Quart Jars	40 minutes

Hot Pack—Prepare peas, and cover with boiling water. Heat to boiling, and drain. Pack hot to within 1¼ inches from top for pints and 1½ inches for quarts. Do not pack tightly. Add salt, and cover with boiling water to within ½ inch from top. Process at 10 pounds pressure for same time as raw pack. Remove jars from canner, and complete seals if necessary.

Peas, Fresh Green

Prepare only fresh, tender young green peas. Shell and wash peas.

Raw Pack—Pack peas into jars to within 1 inch from top. Do not pack tightly. Add salt, and cover with boiling water. Process at 10 pounds pressure:

Pint and Half-Pint Jars	40 minutes
Quart Jars	40 minutes

Hot Pack—Cover shelled peas with boiling water, and return to boil. Pack hot into jars to within 1 inch from top. Add salt, and cover with boiling water. Process at 10 pounds pressure for same time as raw pack. Remove jars from canner and complete seals if necessary.

Potatoes

Wash and pare potatoes. Cut into ½ inch cubes, or leave small potatoes whole. Boil cubes for 2 minutes and small whole potatoes for 10 minutes. Pack hot into jars leaving ½ inch headspace, add salt, and cover with boiling water. Process at 10 pounds pressure:

Pint and Half-Pint Jars	35 minutes
Quart Jars	40 minutes

Pumpkin and Winter Squash

Wash, remove seeds, and peel. Cut into 1 inch cubes.

Hot Pack Only—Barely cover pumpkin with boiling water, and cook one minute. Pack hot into jars to within ½ inch from top. Add salt, and cover with boiling liquid. Process at 10 pounds pressure:

Pint and Half-Pint Jars	55 minutes
Quart Jars	90 minutes

Pumpkin or Winter Squash, Strained

Wash, remove seeds and fibrous material, and peel. Cut into cubes or strips, and steam until tender. Press through strainer, or run through food mill.

Hot Pack Only—Reheat strained pumpkin until heated through. Pack into jars to within ½ inch from top, adding no salt or liquid. Process at 10 pounds pressure:

Pint and Half-Pint Jars	65 minutes
Quart Jars	80 minutes

Left, to raw pack squash, pack prepared pieces into jars. *Right,* cover with boiling water and process in pressure canner.

Squash, Summer

Wash but do not peel squash; trim ends. Cut into ½ inch slices.

Raw Pack—Pack into jars to within 1 inch from top. Add salt, and cover with boiling water to within ½ inch from top. Process at 10 pounds pressure.

Pint and Half-Pint Jars	25 minutes
Quart Jars	30 minutes

Hot Pack—Just cover prepared squash with boiling water, and bring to boiling. Pack hot into jars to within ½ inch from top. Add salt, and cover with hot cooking liquid. Process at 10 pounds pressure:

Pint and Half-Pint Jars	30 minutes
Quart Jars	40 minutes

Squash, Winter—See Pumpkin.

Sweet Potatoes—Wash.

Dry Pack—Boil or steam until soft; then remove skins and cut into pieces. Pack hot into jars to within 1 inch from top. Add no salt or liquid. Process at 10 pounds pressure:

Pint and Half-Pint Jars	65 minutes
Quart Jars	95 minutes

Wet Pack—Boil or steam sweet potatoes until skins will slip off. Remove skins and cut into pieces. Pack hot into jars to within 1 inch from top. Add salt, and cover with boiling water or a light or medium syrup. Process at 10 pounds pressure:

Pint and Half-Pint Jars	55 minutes
Quart Jars	90 minutes

MEATS

Meats such as beef, pork, lamb, poultry, game birds, and game animals may all be canned using a steam-pressure canner. Meats must be canned in this method utilizing the proper equipment and methods to insure against the possibility of botulism poisoning. Make sure you follow directions carefully, and don't take any short cuts, reduce processing times, or process at below 240°F. Use the directions with your particular pressure canner.

Meat to be canned should be only good quality and well-chilled. Make sure you keep meat well-chilled during the preparations for canning. If using frozen meat, allow it to thaw in a refrigerator at 40°F or lower until almost all of the ice crystals have disappeared.

To reduce the bacteria and chance of spoilage, make sure everything including equipment and work area is spotlessly clean. Cutting boards and other wooden surfaces should be washed in a diluted solution of liquid chlorine disinfectant, such as directed on the container, and then washed off with boiling water.

Wash pressure canner thoroughly in hot soapy water; however, don't put a lid with a dial in the water. Then wipe or rinse with clean, hot water. Make sure the petcock and valve or weighted gauge are operating properly. If you're using a weighted gauge at a high altitude, make sure it is working properly. If you have a dial gauge, have it checked before each canning season and at least once during the season if you can a lot. Check with manufacturer, dealer, or county extension agent as to where to have it checked.

It's a good idea to use a thermometer both when hot-packing meat and when exhausting air from jars of cold-packed meats. In this method, you'll be sure the meat has been properly heated to 170°F, which is needed to exhaust air from the jars. Place the thermometer directly in the center of the jar that is being heated, with the bulb about halfway to the bottom of the container. If you don't have a thermometer, follow directions and heat the meat for the specific times given.

When hot-packing meat, you will be covering the meat or poultry with a broth. To make the broth, place bony pieces of meat in a pan and add water to cover. Simmer until meat falls from bones; then skim the fat from the top, and remove the bones from the broth. The boiling broth is added to the containers holding the precooked meat. It should be added to fill the containers to the level that is required by the directions.

Meat should be packed fairly loosely in the jars to insure that all is heated throughout. If the jars are filled too full during the processing, the meat will spew out and lose some liquid. When filling jars with meat, use only one jar at a time, making sure you keep the precooked meat hot during packing.

Again, there are two basic methods utilized for processing meats, one of which is raw pack—the meat is packed into the jars uncooked. In this method, the jars are heated to 170°F to exhaust or remove all air from the jars before processing in the steam-pressure canner. In the hot pack method, the meat is precooked, and then packed hot into the jars. The boiling broth is poured over the meat; then the containers are placed in the canner and processed according to directions. Again, the meat should be heated to 170°F at the time the jars are sealed to make sure all air is exhausted. Air *must* be exhausted for all raw-packed meats except meat and vegetable combinations and raw-packed poultry with the bones left on. Follow the directions carefully for preparing each different meat.

Exhausting or removing air from jars is done by placing the jars packed with raw meat on a metal rack in a large pan of boiling water, with the water level about 2 inches below the jar tops. Place a thermometer in the center jar, cover the pan, and bring water to a boil. Boil slowly until the temperature at the center of the center jar is 170°F. Or if you don't have a thermometer, follow the time suggested to cook meat to medium done. The heating causes the air to be driven out, and a vacuum is formed to help preserve the flavor of the meat.

Salt is added to canned meat at the same rate that it is added to vegetables—½ teaspoon for pints and 1 teaspoon for quarts. However, salt in these small amounts is not a preservative, merely a flavoring. Meats may be canned salt-free if desired.

The one thing you have to make sure of when canning meats is that all fat is cut away. It's a good idea not to use meats that have too much fat, because any fat on the rims of the jars will prevent them from sealing properly. Fat can also give a rancid taste to the canned meat. So make sure you wipe all jar rims before sealing.

> *NOTE:* Be sure to boil all home-canned meat 20 minutes in a covered container before tasting. Be alert for spoilage at all times. Darkened lids or meat is not necessarily a sign of spoilage.

DIRECTIONS FOR CANNING MEATS

The following directions can be used for beef, veal, pork, lamb, mutton, and large game animals. Slice tender cuts of meat such as loin into lengths 1 inch shorter than jars. Less tender cuts of meat can be cut into chunks and used later for stews, casseroles, etc. Remove bones from larger cuts of meat, and make soup stock or broth from the bony pieces.

Left, the first step in raw packing meats is to clean the meat, then remove all bones. *Right,* then cut meat into jar-length pieces or into uniform chunks.

Hot Pack—Precook meat slowly in a shallow pan, adding only enough water to keep it from sticking. Cover the pan and stir occasionally so that the meat will heat evenly. Cook until medium done or until centers of meat pieces reach 170°F. Pack hot meat into jars leaving 1 inch headspace. Add salt, and cover with boiling broth. Process at 10 pounds pressure:

| Pint Jars | 75 minutes |
| Quart Jars | 90 minutes |

Raw Pack—Cut meat as mentioned above, and pack loosely into jars leaving 1 inch headspace. Exhaust air by cooking raw meat in jars to 170°F or until medium done, or for about 75 minutes. Add salt but no liquid. Process at 10 pounds pressure:

| Pint Jars | 75 minutes |
| Quart Jars | 90 minutes |

Ground Meat

Grind fresh meat, keeping the mixture on the lean side. Add 1 teaspoon salt for each pound of ground meat, and mix well. Make patties of a size to fit your widemouth jars. Precook patties in a 325°F oven until medium done; a little pink will still show in the center. Drain patties and discard fat. Pack patties into jars leaving 1 inch headspace, and cover with boiling broth. Process at 10 pounds pressure:

| Pint Jars | 75 minutes |
| Quart Jars | 90 minutes |

Top left, to exhaust air from the jars, set the open, filled jars of meat on a rack in a pan of boiling water. Water should be about 2 inches below jar rims. Insert a thermometer into the center of a jar of meat, cover pan, and heat slowly until thermometer registers 170°F; or cover pan and heat slowly for 75 minutes. *Top right,* remove jars, add salt and lids. *Middle left,* place jars in a pressure canner. *Middle right,* process meats at 10 pounds pressure 75 minutes for pint jars and 90 minutes for quart jars. *Bottom left,* let pressure drop naturally, then open cover tilting the lid away from your face. *Bottom right,* place jars on a rack to cool, then wash jars, remove rings, label and store.

Pork Sausage

Prepare and grind fresh pork, again keeping it on the lean side. Add your favorite seasonings; however, use them sparingly as the flavor increases when canned. Sage should be omitted as it does not can well. Shape patties and precook, pack, and process as for ground meat.

Corned Beef

Prepare corned beef as directed in Chapter 8. Remove meat from brine, and wash thoroughly. Cut into jar-size pieces. Cover meat with cold water and bring to a boil. If broth is extremely salty, drain meat and bring to boil again with fresh cold water. Pack hot meat into jars leaving 1 inch headspace. Cover with boiling broth or fresh boiling water (if still salty). Process at 10 pounds pressure:

Pint Jars	75 minutes
Quart Jars	90 minutes

DIRECTIONS FOR CANNING CHICKEN

The following directions for chicken can be used for ducks, turkey, geese, guinea, squab, rabbit, and small game animals. They can all be prepared with bones or without. Prepare a canning broth for poultry in the same manner as the beef broth, using bony pieces of chicken.

Left, to prepare chickens for hot pack canning, rinse meat and wipe dry, then disjoint the bird. First remove legs, thighs and wings. *Right,* cut between the ribs from the breastbone to the backbone. Break backbone in half.

Top right, cut down through breast around the wishbone. *Top left,* remove breast meat from both sides of center bone. *Middle left,* separate drumstick and thigh, then cover meat with hot water or broth and precook meat until medium done. *Middle right,* pack hot chicken into jars, placing thighs and drumsticks with skin side out around sides of jar and breast meat in the center. Cover meat with boiling broth leaving 1 inch headspace. *Bottom left,* wipe jar rims, add lids and process in pressure canner at 10 pounds pressure 65 minutes for pint jars and 75 minutes for quart jars of chicken with bones. *Bottom right,* cool jars on racks, then wash, remove rings and label.

Hot Pack (With Bones)—Bone the breast, and cut drumsticks shorter. Place meat in a pan, and cover with hot broth. Cover pan and cook until meat is medium done; pink should be almost gone from center. Pack legs and thighs with skin side next to jar around the outside of the jar. Pack the breast meat in the center. Fill in with other pieces. Leave 1 inch headspace, add salt, and cover with boiling broth. Process at 10 pounds pressure:

Pint Jars	65 minutes
Quart Jars	75 minutes

Hot Pack (Without Bones)—Cut up poultry and remove bones but not skin; then precook as above. Or you can precook and then remove bones. Pack hot meat into jars in the same manner as above, again leaving 1 inch headspace, adding salt, and covering with boiling broth. Process at 10 pounds pressure:

Pint Jars	75 minutes
Quart Jars	90 minutes

Raw Pack (With Bones)—Cut up and prepare poultry as for the hot pack. Pack the raw pieces into jars in the same manner. Leave 1 inch headspace, and add salt. Do not exhaust or add liquid. Process at 10 pounds pressure:

Quart Jars	80 minutes

Raw Pack (Without Bones)—Prepare poultry and remove bones but not skin. Pack raw into jars as before, and leave 1 inch headspace. Exhaust air by cooking at a slow boil until the poultry reaches 170°F in the center of the jar, or for about 75 minutes. Add salt, adjust lids, and process at 10 pounds pressure:

Pint Jars	75 minutes
Quart Jars	90 minutes

DIRECTIONS FOR CANNING FISH

Clean fish (except salmon) and cut into jar-length pieces. Soak 1 hour in a brine of 1 cup salt to 1 gallon water. Drain well, and pack into jars. Leave 1 inch headspace, and add salt. Do not add liquid. Process at 10 pounds pressure:

Pint and Quart Jars	100 minutes

Top left, cut fish into jar length pieces or into chunks and pack into jars; no need to remove bones. *Top right*, add salt to each jar, *Side*, process in a pressure canner.

Salmon

Clean fish and remove head, fins, and tail. Slowly pour hot water over the fish; do not break the skin. Scrape until skin is clean and white. Cut into jar-length pieces, and pack into jars. Add salt, and leave 1 inch headspace. Do not add liquid. Process at 10 pounds pressure:

Pint and Quart Jars   100 minutes

Clams

Scrub clams, and steam to open shells. Remove from shells, and save juice. Boil clams 5 minutes in salted water; then drain and pack, leaving 1 inch headspace. Cover with juice, adding boiling water if necessary. Process at 10 pounds pressure:

Pint and Quart Jars   90 minutes

Shrimp

Wash freshly caught shrimp in cold water; then drain. Boil shrimp for 8 to 10 minutes in a brine of 1 pound salt to 1 gallon water. Drain and rinse in cold water. Shell and devein shrimp. Pack quickly into jars leaving 1 inch headspace. Cover shrimp with a boiling brine solution containing 1 teaspoon salt to each quart water. Shrimp can also be packed dry. Process at 10 pounds pressure:

Pint and Quart Jars   90 minutes

2

FREEZING FRUITS, VEGETABLES, AND MEATS

Freezing food is one of the most popular methods of food preservation, probably because it's the easiest, and the food tastes "almost fresh." Freezing not only preserves the taste, flavor, and nutrition in food but results in foods much quicker and easier to prepare for the table. Most of the preparation is done before freezing.

Freezing does not kill the bacteria that causes food to spoil; it only halts the activity of the bacteria during the freezing stage (or at 0°F). If at any time the temperature of the food goes above 5°F, the quality of the food will be less.

Freezing, however, is not the most economical method of food preservation. It is also not necessarily the best method of preservation for all foods. For instance, vegetables that are to be eaten raw will lose much of their body and taste compared to their fresh counterparts. On the other hand, meats and such vegetables as corn, lima beans, and almost all fruits are best frozen rather than preserved by other means. They retain much more of their flavor and original texture when frozen. Although freezing is the simplest and easiest method, it just isn't feasible for large quantities of some foods, especially those with a lot of bulk.

Frozen food won't keep indefinitely as will foods utilizing other methods of food preservation. Most food will start to lose taste and nutrition and will become freezer burned or "dried out" if stored for longer than a year. Some foods such as pork will become rancid and lose flavor if stored for longer than 6 to 8 months.

Foods must be frozen as soon after harvesting or preparing as possible; "quick freeze" them as soon as possible. If you're doing fruits or vegetables, pick only a small batch at a time, early in the morning if possible. Prepare a small batch, placing each container of food in your refrigerator to allow it to cool while you prepare others. Then place a few packages at a time in the freezer so they will freeze quickly and properly. One of the biggest mistakes in home freezing is in placing too much unfrozen food in the freezer at one time. This not only prevents proper "fast freezing" of the freshly prepared food but may warm the freezer enough to damage food that is already stored in it. The basic rule of thumb is to place no more than 2 to 3 pounds of fresh food in the freezer for each cubic foot of freezer capacity. Place the packages around the sides or against the freezer coils, and leave an air space between them. If your particular unit has a fast-freezing section, use it for this process. After the packages of food have frozen solid, they can be rearranged so they are stacked more closely together and other unfrozen packages added.

Make up a list of the quantities of the various foods as you place them in the freezer. As you remove foods for use, mark them off the list. In this way, you'll know exactly how many packages of each food you have in the freezer, and you won't have to keep digging through the freezer to see how many packages of lima beans or strawberries you have left. It is also a good idea to place the latest frozen items on the bottom of the freezer or to the back, depending on the style of freezer, bringing the older foods to the top or front so they can be used first.

Foods that are stored for a long time actually become quite expensive when you figure the cost of operating the unit. The quicker you can use and replace foods from the freezer, the better the taste of the food, as well as the economy.

Like most methods of preservation, freezing won't enhance poor quality food. Use only good quality foods, and keep the utensils and food preparation area clean during processing. Have everything organized and ready to work before you gather or purchase food. Use only recommended containers, and pack as directed.

EQUIPMENT

There are basically two types of home freezers, in addition to locker space, which is rented from a locker plant and works well for those who can't afford the initial cost of a freezer or don't have the space to keep one. In the long run, the freezer at home will work the best. It should be placed as close to the kitchen as possible for easy access. Both home freezers have advantages and disadvantages. An upright freezer won't hold as much food but is somewhat easier to get into. The chest-type freezer holds more food but is somewhat harder to get into, especially for older people. The uprights range in size from 6 to 22 cubic feet and normally have several shelves on which to place the food. Chest-type freezers normally run a bit larger, from 6 to 32 cubic feet, and the better ones have baskets that can be suspended down in the freezer enabling you to keep foods more organized. Another type of freezer is the combination freezer-refrigerator. Although this is great for keeping

Keep a thermometer in your freezer and check often to make sure the temperature stays below 0°F.

a few frozen items handy in the kitchen, it is not large enough to hold a great deal of frozen food. It normally runs from 3 to 16 cubic feet.

Regardless of the style of freezer, place a thermometer inside near the top, and make sure the freezer maintains a 0°F or −10°F temperature. If your freezer is frost-free, all you'll have to do is wipe it clean once a year with a bit of water and baking soda. The nonfrost-free models should be defrosted at least once a year or when the ice on the sides builds up to ¾ of an inch. Try to pick a time when food supply is low in the freezer. Remove all food, wrap it in old blankets or quilts, and place pans of hot water in the freezer to melt the ice. Again wash down with water and baking soda, then wipe clean.

CONTAINERS

There are literally hundreds of different containers that can be used for freezer containers; the main thing to remember is to suit the container to the food. For instance, paper wrapping is fine for solid materials but naturally won't work for liquids. In addition to the make-do containers that are recycled from purchased foods, there are several standard types of freezer containers.

All freezer containers should prevent the food from drying out, be easy to seal, be waterproof, and must not be brittle or they will crack or break at low temperatures. They should also be vapor-proof to prevent evaporation of liquid. Rigid freezer containers of glass and plastic are vapor-proof, while freezer bags, paper, and wrapping materials are vapor resistant if used properly. Most recycled items such as the cartons of milk, cottage cheese, and whipped cream are not vapor resistant. Make sure the container you select will hold enough food for one meal for your family.

Glass Jars. Glass jars that can be used in the freezer are normally called "can or freeze jars" and have sides that flare out slightly at the top. This enables you to more easily remove semifrozen foods. The metal lids are simply screwed down in place and may be reused as many times as desired.

Plastic Freezer Containers. These boxes are made especially for freezer use from a tough durable plastic. They are straight-sided and slightly tapered to the bottom. The flat bottom and recessed top lid ease stacking. Lids are snapped down over the edges of the container. With care, these will last for years.

The newer glass jars on the market are called *can* or *freeze* jars and can be used in the freezer as well as for canning.

Nonrigid Freezer Containers. Many foods can simply be packed in plastic bags or wrapped securely in paper. Bags made of heavy cellophane, aluminum foil, or polyethylene may be used for packing almost any food. The bags may become a bit awkward to stack and handle if they freeze in unusual shapes. Placing them in a heavy, waxed cardboard carton during freezing will help shape the bags so they can be stored more easily. Heavy-duty plastic wrap and freezer paper can be used to protect meats. They should be double wrapped, first in the plastic wrap, then followed by the heavy freezer paper. Individual servings of hamburger, etc., may be separated by pieces of waxed paper and then wrapped together to make up enough to serve your family.

Plastic bags are normally sealed by tying with a twist-on and then folding over and twisting again, or by sealing a special edge that snaps together. You can also heat-seal bags by laying a bit of heat-resistant material over the edges of the bag and using a warm iron, or by using one of the newer heat-seal bag machines.

Paper is held in place by a special freezer tape that will hold the paper in place even at low, dry temperatures.

Remember, grocery packaging is not sufficient to protect foods for more than a few days in the freezer. If you don't plan to use frozen vegetables or meats immediately, add an additional wrapping of freezer paper to the store package, or simply place the store package in a plastic bag and seal.

PACKING INTO CONTAINERS

It's a good idea to pack the food into the containers while cold, placing them immediately in the freezer, or in the refrigerator until you can place them in the freezer. This helps the freezing process and retains color, flavor, etc.

The foods should be packed down tightly to remove all air, but be careful not to bruise or crush foods other than those you desire to be crushed.

Make sure you allow for proper headspace as shown in the following table. As food expands when frozen, this headspace prevents the possibility of food spewing out of the package during freezing. When sealing the container, make sure you remove as much air as possible. In bags, press out air before making seal.

Head space to allow between packed food and closure

TYPE OF PACK	Container with wide top opening[1]		Container with narrow top opening[2]	
	Pint	Quart	Pint	Quart
Liquid pack (Fruit packed in juice, sugar, syrup, or water; crushed or puree; juice.)	½ inch	1 inch	¾ inch[3]	1½ inches
Dry pack[4] (Fruit or vegetable packed without added sugar or liquid.)	½ inch	½ inch	½ inch	½ inch

[1]This is head space for tall containers—either straight or slightly flared.
[2]Glass canning jars may be used for freezing most fruits and vegetables except those packed in water.
[3]Head space for juice should be 1½ inches.
[4]Vegetables that pack loosely, such as broccoli and asparagus, require no head space.

FREEZING FRUITS

Most fruits freeze well, but the various fruits do require somewhat different methods of preparation. Some can be frozen whole; others need to be sliced, peeled, made into puree, etc. Normally, fruits are better if they're prepared and sweetened before they're frozen. Then it's merely a matter of allowing them to thaw out before serving or cooking. Again, poor quality fruits won't improve when frozen. The fruit must be fully ripe and mature. If the fruit is somewhat green, spread out on trays in a clean, airy place, and allow to ripen thoroughly. Fruits may also darken or become soft if left too long from ripening to the freezing stage, so when you're ready to prepare for freezing, move rapidly, and do only small batches at a time.

Before packing into the containers, the fruits must be prepared. All fruits should be washed in cold running water. Wash only a small quantity at a time so you won't bruise or crush such fruits as berries. It's a good idea to place a wire basket in the sink and wash in that, then merely lift the basket from the sink to allow the water to drain away.

The fruits shouldn't be allowed to soak in the water, because they may lose some of their color, flavor, and nutrition.

Galvanized or iron utensils should not be used with fruit or fruit juices, because the acid in the fruit will dissolve the zinc from the coating. By the same token, iron utensils may cause the fruit to darken. Use only plastic, glass, stainless steel, aluminum, or earthenware utensils.

To prepare fruit for freezing, follow directions with individual suggestions for peeling, pitting, or slicing. For fruits that are to be crushed use a potato masher, large slotted spoon, or a food chopper. For making purees you'll need a colander and strainer.

In most cases, fruits will be packed in a sugar or syrup sweetening; however, some fruits may be packed without the addition of sweetening. The selection of the type of packing or the choice of not using one is dependent on the type of fruit. Fruits that are used primarily for desserts should be packed with syrup sweetening. Fruits that will be cooked can be packed without sweetening or in sugar pack.

SYRUP PACK

To make up a syrup pack, dissolve the sugar in warm water or fruit juice until clear. A 40% syrup is used for most fruits. The chart indicates the amounts of sugar and water to make up the various syrups. In packing, the syrup is allowed to cool or is chilled in the refrigerator. Pour only enough into the container to cover the fruit. It normally takes about a half of a cup of syrup to each pint of fruit.

Syrups for use in freezing fruits

Type of syrup	Sugar[1]	Water	Yield of syrup
	Cups	Cups	Cups
30-percent syrup	2	4	5
35-percent syrup	2½	4	5⅓
40-percent syrup	3	4	5½
50-percent syrup	4¾	4	6½
60-percent syrup	7	4	7¾
65-percent syrup	8¾	4	8⅔

[1]In general, up to one-fourth of the sugar may be replaced by corn syrup. A larger proportion of corn syrup may be used if a very bland, light-colored type is selected.

SUGAR PACK

Fruits such as peaches, strawberries, plums, cherries, and seeded grapes will make their own juice if they are placed in the container in layers between layers of sugar. Or place the fruit into a bowl or small pan and sprinkle with sugar. (Use amount given for each individual fruit.) Mix lightly with a large spoon. When sugar is dissolved and juice comes out, ladle into containers. Or place fruit and sugar in layers and allow to stand for about 15 minutes until juice appears and sugar dissolves. Another method for some whole fruits is to coat or dust with sugar and freeze whole. A bit of ascorbic acid may be added if needed.

UNSWEETENED PACK

Fruits such as raspberries, blackberries, blueberries, and rhubarb will freeze quite easily without the addition of sugar. The fruits are simply placed in the container without sweetening. They may also be covered with water to which a bit of ascorbic acid has been added, or the fruits may be packed and crushed to produce their own juice.

DARKENING OF FRUITS

It's natural for some fruits (peaches, apples, and pears) to darken or discolor during freezing. To prevent this, the fruit should be pretreated by peeling, slicing, etc., then quickly dropping into a solution made of 1 teaspoon ascorbic acid and 1 tablespoon of citric acid to 1 gallon of cold water. Or follow ascorbic acid manufacturer's directions. Other methods of preventing discoloration of fruit is by using the juice of citrus fruits such as lemons; however, it takes quite a bit of lemon juice to prevent discoloration. Some fruits may be steamed before freezing to prevent discoloration. To prevent the top layer of fruit from becoming exposed to air and discoloring, you can crumple up a piece of freezer paper and place it over the fruit in the container.

To determine how much frozen food you'll get from fresh food, follow the accompanying table.

Approximate yield of frozen fruits from fresh

Fruit	Fresh, as Purchased or Picked	Frozen
Apples	1 bu. (48 lb.)	32 to 40 pt.
	1 box (44 lb.)	29 to 35 pt.
	1¼ to 1½ lb.	1 pt.
Apricots	1 bu. (48 lb.)	60 to 72 pt.
	1 crate (22 lb.)	28 to 33 pt.
	⅔ to ⅘ lb.	1 pt.
Berries[1]	1 crate (24 qt.)	32 to 36 pt.
	1⅓ to 1½ pt.	1 pt.
Cantaloupes	1 dozen (28 lb.)	22 pt.
	1 to 1¼ lb.	1 pt.
Cherries, sweet or sour	1 bu. (56 lb.)	36 to 44 pt.
	1¼ to 1½ lb.	1 pt.
Cranberries	1 box (25 lb.)	50 pt.
	1 peck (8 lb.)	16 pt.
	½ lb.	1 pt.
Currants	2 qt. (3 lb.)	4 pt.
	¾ lb.	1 pt.
Peaches	1 bu. (48 lb.)	32 to 48 pt.
	1 lug box (20 lb.)	13 to 20 pt.
	1 to 1½ lb.	1 pt.
Pears	1 bu. (50 lb.)	40 to 50 pt.
	1 western box (46 lb.)	37 to 46 pt.
	1 to 1¼ lb.	1 pt.
Pineapple	5 lb.	4 pt.
Plums and prunes	1 bu. (56 lb.)	38 to 56 pt.
	1 crate (20 lb.)	13 to 20 pt.
	1 to 1½ lb.	1 pt.
Raspberries	1 crate (24 pt.)	24 pt.
	1 pt.	1 pt.
Rhubarb	15 lb.	15 to 22 pt.
	⅔ to 1 lb.	1 pt.
Strawberries	1 crate (24 qt.)	38 pt.
	⅔ qt.	1 pt.

[1]Includes blackberries, blueberries, boysenberries, dewberries, elderberries, gooseberries, huckleberries, loganberries, and youngberries.

When serving frozen fruits raw, thaw only to the ice crystal stage. If they are allowed to thaw completely, some fruits, especially soft fruits such as strawberries, will become mushy and not quite as juicy tasting. Allow fruit to thaw in a sealed container in the refrigerator. A jar of frozen fruit can be thawed more quickly by setting under cold running water.

Below are specific directions for preparing different fruits for the freezer:

Apples

Wash, peel, core, and slice firm, crisp apples. To prevent darkening, slice apples into a solution of ¼ cup salt to 1 gallon of water. When all apples are sliced, drain and then rinse in clear water; drain again. (Do not leave apples in solution over 20 minutes.) Pack apples as is with no sweetening, or add ½ cup sugar for each quart of apple slices for a sugar pack, or cover apples with a 40% syrup for a syrup pack. If using a syrup pack, add ½ teaspoon crystalline ascorbic acid to each quart of syrup, and slice apples directly into syrup, thus eliminating the saltwater soak.

Applesauce

Wash, core, and slice apples. Cook over a low heat until apples are soft, adding only enough water to keep the apples from sticking. Press apples through sieve, and sweeten if desired. Pack into containers allowing for headspace; label, date, and freeze.

An uncooked applesauce which is delicious frozen can be prepared using a food mill as described in Chapter 3. Wash, core, and chunk apples. Run through food mill. Pack, label, date, and freeze. This kind of applesauce should be frozen to retain that fresh, uncooked taste.

Apricots

Peel, halve, and pit fully ripe but sound apricots. To peel, dip in boiling water for 20 seconds and then cool in cold water. Apricots can be frozen in halves, slices, or pureed. To freeze slices or halves in syrup, prepare them directly into a 40% syrup to which ½ teaspoon crystalline ascorbic acid has been added to each quart. To pack in sugar, mix ¼ teaspoon crystalline ascorbic acid and ½ to 1 cup sugar with each quart of fruit. For a delicious topping, crush the apricots adding ¼ teaspoon crystalline ascorbic acid and 1 to 1⅓ cups sugar to each quart crushed apricots. Pack, label, date, and freeze.

Avocados

Peel, pit, and mash. Add ⅛ teaspoon crystalline ascorbic acid to each quart mashed fruit. Pack, label, date, and freeze.

Blackberries

Stem and sort berries; then carefully wash in cold water. Blackberries can be frozen without sugar or with ¾ cup sugar added to each quart of berries or by covering berries with a 40% syrup. Add 1 cup sugar to each quart of crushed berries.

Blueberries (Huckleberries)

Sort, wash, and drain. Freeze unsweetened for use in muffins, etc., or add 1 cup sugar to each quart berries, or cover with 40% syrup.

Boysenberries

Follow directions for Blackberries.

Cherries, Sour

Wash, stem, and pit. Mix 1 cup sugar with each quart fruit, or cover with 60% syrup. Unsweetened frozen cherries lose color and flavor rapidly.

Cherries, Sweet

Wash, stem, and pit. Add ½ teaspoon crystalline ascorbic acid to each quart fruit, and sweeten with 1 cup sugar or cover with a 40% syrup.

Coconut

Puncture eye of coconut; drain and save milk. Shred, chop, or grind meat, pack into containers, and cover with milk. Add ½ cup sugar to each quart of coconut if desired.

Cranberries

Sort, wash, and drain. Pack into containers and freeze. Or cook for cranberry sauce, and then freeze.

Currants

Sort, stem, and wash. Pack into containers without sugar, or add ¾ cup sugar to each quart, or cover with a 50% syrup.

Dates

Wash, halve, and remove pits. Freeze as halves or chop or grind. Add no sugar.

Dewberries

Follow directions for Blackberries.

Elderberries

Follow directions for Blueberries.

Figs

Sort, wash, and stem. Pack peeled, unpeeled, whole, sliced, or crushed. Freeze without sugar, covered with a 35% to 40% syrup, or add 1 cup sugar to each quart of fruit. Add only ⅔ cup sugar to each quart of crushed fruit.

Fruit Cocktail

Prepare fruits according to individual instructions, and mix, covering with a 40% syrup. Add ½ teaspoon ascorbic acid to each quart of syrup if needed for the particular fruits. Remember, berries will soften and color the mixture.

Gooseberries

Sort, stem, and wash. Pack into containers, and freeze.

Grapefruit

Peel grapefruit, and separate into sections. Remove all white membrane and seeds. Pack grapefruit in its own juice and freeze, or cover with a 40% syrup (using juice to make the syrup).

Grapes

Stem, sort, and wash. Halve, and remove seeds if necessary. Pack into containers, and cover with 40% syrup.

Huckleberries

See Blueberries.

Loganberries

Follow directions for Blackberries.

Melons (Cantaloupes, Honeydew, Muskmelons, and Watermelons)

Cut ripe melons in halves, and remove seeds. Cut melons into 1 inch cubes or slices, or make balls. Pack into containers and cover with a 30% syrup.

Nectarines

Wash and pit fruit. Then slice, quarter, or halve. Cover with a 40% syrup with ½ teaspoon crystalline ascorbic acid added to each quart, or add ½ teaspoon crystalline ascorbic acid and 1 cup sugar to each quart of prepared fruit. Or you can crush the fruit and add 1 to 1⅓ cups sugar to each cup of crushed fruit.

Oranges

Prepare as for Grapefruit.

Peaches

To peel, dip a few at a time in boiling water for 20 seconds or until skins loosen. Cool quickly in ice water. Peel, halve, and pit peaches;

Top left, scald peaches to peel, or pit and peel by hand for a firmer, more attractive product. *Top right,* pour ½ cup cold syrup into containers and slice peaches directly into containers. *Bottom left,* add more syrup to cover peaches leaving ½ inch headspace for widemouth pint containers. *Bottom right,* a crumpled piece of waxed paper placed on top of the peaches will keep them in the syrup and from darkening.

then slice into a 40% syrup to which ½ teaspoon crystalline ascorbic acid has been added to each quart. Or mix ⅔ cup sugar and ¼ teaspoon crystalline ascorbic acid with each quart of fruit. Pureed peaches are prepared by crushing the fruit and adding 1 cup sugar and ⅛ teaspoon crystalline ascorbic acid to each quart of crushed fruit.

Pears

These are better if canned but can be frozen by peeling, quartering, and removing the cores. Pack in a 40% syrup with ½ teaspoon crystalline ascorbic acid added per quart of syrup or by adding 1 cup sugar and ½ teaspoon crystalline ascorbic acid to each quart of fruit.

Persimmons

Wash and press soft ripe fruit through a sieve. Add 1/8 teaspoon crystalline ascorbic acid to each quart of fruit puree. Native persimmons need no sugar; however, cultivated varieties can be frozen with 1 cup of sugar added to each quart of puree.

Pineapple

Pare and core pineapple, being sure to remove eyes; then slice, dice, or crush fruit. Freeze pineapple in its own juice or in a 40% syrup made with fruit juice, or add 1 cup sugar to each 4 cups of fruit.

Plums

Pit regular plums and prune plums, and leave whole or cut in halves or quarters. They can be frozen without sugar, water, or syrup; they can be covered with a 40% syrup with 1/2 teaspoon crystalline ascorbic acid added per quart; or you can add 1 cup sugar and the acid to each quart of fruit.

Raspberries

Prepare as for Blackberries.

Rhubarb

Wash, trim, and cut in 1 inch pieces. Pack and freeze dry, or cover with a 40% syrup, or add 1 cup sugar to each quart of rhubarb. Rhubarb can also be made into a sauce before freezing.

Strawberries

Sort, wash, and hull berries; then slice. Pack into containers; cover with a 40% to 50% syrup; or gently mix 1/2 to 3/4 cup sugar with each quart of berries. Berries can also be frozen whole in a dry pack with no sugar or syrup. For strawberry puree, mix 1/2 to 3/4 cup sugar with each quart of crushed or strained berries.

Top left, wash berries in cold water by lifting the berries from the water rather than pouring the water off the berries; drain. *Top right,* remove stems, then slice. *Middle left,* sprinkle sugar over berries and turn gently until berries are coated and juice forms. *Middle right,* pack berries into containers leaving ½ inch headspace for widemouth pint containers. *Bottom,* add lids; then label and freeze.

To wash vegetables for freezing, place the vegetables in a large container or the sink. Cover with cold water and stir to help loosen dirt. Lift the vegetables from the water and drain.

Youngberries

Prepare as for Blackberries.

FREEZING VEGETABLES

The cardinal rule when freezing vegetables, like most foods, is to choose only fresh, tender vegetables—if possible, freshly picked from the garden. All vegetables other than podded vegetables, such as green peas and lima beans, etc. should first be washed in cold running water. Then, using a mesh basket, lift them up out of the water allowing the grit to settle to the bottom of the sink. Sort vegetables according to size, or cut into uniform pieces. Prepare according to information given for individual vegetables.

HEATING

Scalding or *blanching* helps to reduce the action of enzymes and helps to retain the color, flavor, and nutrition of the food. Almost every vegetable except green onions or peppers needs this step before freezing. The best method of blanching for the home canner is to use a blancher, which consists of a blanching basket and cover. Or find a wire basket with a cover that will just fit inside a kettle. To blanch one pound of vegetables, you will need 1 gallon of boiling water in the kettle or blancher. Place the vegetables in the blancher or wire basket, and secure the cover so the vegetables won't float out of the basket when it is lowered

A blancher is the easiest container to use for scalding a large volume of vegetables. The inside basket allows you to remove all the vegetables at the same time after blanching. However, any large container can be used for blanching.

into the boiling water. Lower the vegetables into the boiling water, and start timing immediately.

Each particular vegetable requires a somewhat different blanching time, and it's important that you stick to that time. If you blanch or scald too little, it's worse than if you hadn't gone through the process at all. If you leave the vegetables in the boiling water too long, they will loose color, flavor, and nutrition. Maintain the high heat during the time given for each vegetable. If you live at 5000 feet or more above sea level, you will have to add 1 minute more heat to the instructions given.

Some vegetables may also be blanched by heating in steam rather than boiling water. Vegetables processed in this manner are pumpkin, broccoli, sweet potatoes, and winter squash. For this process, you will need a steam basket and a larger kettle. The vegetables are placed in the steam basket. About an inch of water is placed in a larger kettle, a lid is placed on it, and the vegetables are steamed, keeping them spread out in a single layer in the basket at least 3 inches from the water in the kettle.

Immediately after the vegetables are heated, whether in steam or boiling water, they should be cooled rapidly to halt the cooking process. The best method is to plunge the basket of vegetables into cold water

After blanching, immerse vegetables immediately into cold water and cool them as quickly as possible.

(below 60°F). Keep the water cold by changing frequently or by adding ice. It normally takes about the same amount of time to cool the vegetables as to heat them. Once cool, remove the vegetables from the cold water and allow them to drain.

In almost all instances, vegetables are packed dry or without additional liquid in the containers. However, some feel that the vegetables keep better in the freezer and that more nutrition is preserved if the cooled vegetables are covered with the cooled steaming or blanching water.

The following table gives the estimated amount of frozen vegetables you can expect from a given amount of fresh vegetables.

Pack cooled, drained vegetables into containers, then label and freeze.

Approximate yield of frozen vegetables from fresh

Vegetable	Fresh, as Purchased or Picked	Frozen
Asparagus	1 crate (12 2-lb. bunches)	15 to 22 pt.
	1 to 1½ lb.	1 pt.
Beans, lima (in pods)	1 bu. 32 lb.)	12 to 16 pt.
	2 to 2½ lb.	1 pt.
Beans, snap, green, and wax	1 bu. (30 lb.)	30 to 45 pt.
	⅔ to 1 lb.	1 pt.
Beet greens	15 lb.	10 to 15 pt.
	1 to 1½ lb.	1 pt.
Beets (without tops)	1 bu. (52 lb.)	35 to 42 pt.
	1¼ to 1½ lb.	1 pt.
Broccoli	1 crate (25 lb.)	24 pt.
	1 lb.	1 pt.
Brussels sprouts	4 quart boxes	6 pt.
	1 lb.	1 pt.
Carrots (without tops)	1 bu. (50 lb.)	32 to 40 pt.
	1¼ to 1½ lb.	1 pt.
Cauliflower	2 medium heads	3 pt.
	1⅓ lb.	1 pt.
Chard	1 bu. (12 lb.)	8 to 12 pt.
	1 to 1½ lb.	1 pt.
Collards	1 bu. (12 lb.)	8 to 12 pt.
	1 to 1½ lb.	1 pt.
Corn, sweet (in husks)	1 bu. (35 lb.)	14 to 17 pt.
	2 to 2½ lb.	1 pt.
Kale	1 bu. (18 lb.)	12 to 18 pt.
	1 to 1½ lb.	1 pt.
Mustard greens	1 bu. (12 lb.)	8 to 12 pt.
	1 to 1½ lb.	1 pt.
Peas	1 bu. (30 lb.)	12 to 15 pt.
	2 to 2½ lb.	1 pt.
Peppers, sweet	⅔ lb. (3 peppers)	1 pt.
Pumpkin	3 lb.	2 pt.
Spinach	1 bu. (18 lb.)	12 to 18 pt.
	1 to 1½ lb.	1 pt.
Squash, summer	1 bu. (40 lb.)	1 pt.
	1 to 1¼ lb.	32 to 40 pt.
Squash, winter	3 lb.	2 pt.
Sweet potatoes	⅔ lb.	1 pt.

Below are specific directions for preparing the different vegetables for the freezer:

Asparagus

Pick and freeze only tender, young stalks. Wash in cold water, and remove any woody stems and bracts. Cut stalks into uniform lengths that will fit into your freezing cartons, and sort according to the size of the base of the stalk. Blanch from 2 to 4 minutes depending on the size of the stalk. Chill in ice water; then pack into containers and freeze, adding no liquid to the containers.

Beans, Green and Yellow Wax

Select tender young beans that snap when broken. Wash beans in cold water, and stem. Cut into 1 to 2 inch pieces, leave whole, or slice lengthwise into french-style beans. Blanch 2 to 3 minutes; then plunge into ice water until chilled. Pack into containers, label with type of beans, date, and freeze.

Beans, Italian

Wash and stem; then cut or break into 2 inch pieces. Scald 3 to 4 minutes; then chill and pack.

Beans, Lima

Wash pods and shell, then blanch; or blanch, then shell. Blanch podded limas 1½ to 3 minutes depending on size, and blanch pods 4 minutes. Cool quickly in cold water, and pack into containers. Label, date and freeze.

Beans, Shelled Green

Shell plump, full-podded green beans. Blanch 1 minute; then cool quickly and pack.

Beans, Soy

Select well-filled green pods, and wash in cold water. Blanch pods 5 minutes; then cool in ice water, and shell. Pack and freeze.

Beets

Select small, tender beets and wash well. Leave about 1 inch of the stem in place as well as all the root. Cook until tender. Chill quickly in ice water, and slip skins. Tiny beets can be frozen whole; larger ones should be sliced or diced. Package and freeze.

Broccoli

Select tender heads and stalks. Split lengthwise to make more uniform pieces, and soak in salt water to make sure all insects are removed. Rinse in clear, cold water and drain. Scald 3 to 4 minutes depending on size, and pack into containers.

Brussels Sprouts

Select firm, small sprouts. Soak in salt water to remove all insects; then rinse in clear water and drain. Scald 3 to 5 minutes depending on size, and pack into containers.

Cabbage

Select firm, crisp heads. Remove outer leaves, and shred or cut into small wedges, removing core. Soak in salt water if insects might be present. Blanch 1½ to 2 minutes; then chill quickly. Pack and freeze. Frozen cabbage can only be used in cooked dishes.

Carrots

Select tender, fresh carrots. Remove tops; wash and peel or scrape. Whole small carrots should be blanched 5 minutes, while sliced or diced carrots should be blanched only 2 minutes. Cool quickly in cold water; pack and freeze.

Cauliflower

Select compact, snow-white heads. Cut or break into 1 inch flowerettes, and soak in salt water to remove insects. Rinse in clear water and drain. Scald 3 minutes, then cool quickly in cold water, drain, and pack.

Celery

Trim crisp, tender stalks, and cut into 1 inch pieces. Blanch 3 minutes; then cool quickly in cold water, drain, and pack. Frozen celery can only be used in cooked dishes.

Corn, Sweet

Select only fresh milk-stage corn ready for eating. Remove husks and silks; then wash. Blanch 4 minutes; then cool quickly in cold water, changing water if necessary to cool ears. For whole-kernel corn, cut kernels off close to the cob, but be sure not to get any of the cob. Package and freeze. *For cream-style corn,* cut kernels from the cob about half of the depth of the kernels, and then scrape the cob. Package and freeze. *For corn-on-the-cob,* blanch, cool, and drain thoroughly. Blanch 7 to 10 minutes depending on size of ears. Wrap in freezer paper, or pack into containers.

Eggplant

Select eggplants that have a uniform dark color but are not too mature. Wash, peel, and slice or dice. Scald immediately in boiling water for 4 minutes. To retain color, immediately dip pieces into a solution of 1 quart water and 3 teaspoons citric acid. Finish cooling pieces in cold water, and pack immediately. Package slices for frying by placing two pieces of freezer or waxed paper between each slice of eggplant.

Greens

Select tender, young leaves. Sort through leaves, and remove woody stems. Wash thoroughly. Blanch 1½ to 3 minutes depending on how young and tender the leaves are. Chill immediately in ice water; pack and freeze.

Kohlrabi

Select small- to medium-sized kohlrabi. Wash, remove top and bottom, and peel. Slice or dice, or leave small ones whole. Blanch 1 to 3 minutes depending on size, and chill immediately. Drain and pack.

Mixed Vegetables

Prepare each vegetable separately, scalding the recommended time. Mix after cooling, or pack in layers in containers, adding another layer of a different vegetable as they come in season and can be prepared.

Mushrooms

Select tender, fresh mushrooms. If wild, make sure they are edible. Wash well, and remove end of stem and any imperfect areas. Leave small mushrooms whole, slice, or quarter larger ones. Sauté in butter until almost done, and then cool by setting pan on ice. Package in recipe amounts, and pour any butter left in pan over them. Seal and freeze.

Okra

Select young, tender, green pods. Wash thoroughly, and remove stems without cutting into seeds. Blanch 3 to 5 minutes depending on size, and cool immediately in cold water. Package whole, or slice.

Onions

Clean onions as for the table, and chop fine. Pack into containers and freeze. Small green onions can be done in the same manner.

Parsnips

Select small, tender parsnips that have not turned woody. Remove tops, and peel. Slice lengthwise or crosswise into $\frac{1}{4}$ inch slices, and blanch 2 to 3 minutes. Cool immediately in cold water, drain, and pack.

Peas (Blackeye, Field, Crowder, etc.)

Select well-filled pods that have not started to dry. Shell peas, removing any that are dried or discolored. Scald 2 minutes; then cool immediately. Drain and pack.

Peas, Edible Pod

Select flat pods with good color. Wash, and remove stems, blossom ends, and strings. Blanch 3 minutes; then chill immediately in ice water, drain, and pack.

Peas, Green

Select crisp pods containing tender peas. Wash pods, and then shell peas. Blanch peas 2 minutes; then cool immediately in ice water. Drain peas, pack, and freeze.

Peppers, Green and Hot

Wash peppers, and remove stems and seeds. Dice; pack into small, serving-size bags; then pack smaller bags into a large container.

Peppers, Pimento

Select well-ripened, deep red peppers. Wash, and remove stems and seeds. Roast in a 400°F oven until peels are charred; then cool and pack.

Potatoes, French Fried

Peel potatoes, and cut as french fries. Fry in hot fat until light golden brown. Drain and cool; then package. To serve, warm in oven or broiler.

Potatoes, Sweet

Wash potatoes, and grease skins lightly. Bake in oven until just tender; cool, wrap individually, and freeze. Or prepare candied sweet potatoes and freeze, covering potatoes with candied liquid. You can also bake, mash, and freeze the puree for pies. Add lemon juice to preserve color.

Potatoes, White

New small potatoes can be scraped and blanched 3 to 5 minutes, cooled, packaged and frozen. Larger potatoes can be peeled and diced, then blanched 3 minutes, cooled and packaged.

Pumpkin

Peel pumpkins and remove seeds and stringy area. Cut into uniform pieces and bake, steam or cook in a small amount of water until tender. Press through sieve and cool. Package and freeze or make pumpkin pie filling by your favorite recipe and freeze. Do not freeze cloves in the pie filling.

Rutabagas

Select young, tender rutabagas; remove tops; wash and peel. Cut into cubes, and blanch 2 minutes; then cool, package, and freeze. Or cook until tender, mash, then cool, package, and freeze.

Squash, Summer

Select immature squash with tender skin and seeds. Wash and slice; then scald 3 minutes, cool, package, and freeze.

Squash, Winter

Select fully mature squash with tough, hard shells. Wash, cut or break squash in pieces, and remove seeds and membrane. Bake, boil, or steam until tender. Remove pulp and press through sieve. Cool, package, and freeze.

Tomatoes

Wash, stem, peel, and quarter tomatoes. Pack into containers and freeze. Or tomatoes can be cooked until tender, cooled, then packaged, and frozen.

Tomatoes, Green

To have slices of green tomatoes for frying throughout the winter, remove stems, core tomatoes, and then slice. Package with two pieces of freezer or waxed paper between slices.

Turnips

Wash, remove tops, and peel. Slice, dice, or cook until tender, and mash; then cool, package, and freeze. Blanch 2 to 3 minutes depending on the size of the pieces.

GENERAL DIRECTIONS FOR FREEZING MEATS, POULTRY, FISH, AND DAIRY PRODUCTS

Freezing is the best method of preservation for meats. It keeps the meat fresh tasting and stops deterioration of flavor, nutrition, and color. It is also the easiest and probably the most used method of meat preservation today!

Like all other foods, meats won't be improved by the freezing process. If you use poor quality meats for freezing, you'll get poor results. Regardless of whether you slaughter at home, or raise the animal and have it slaughtered at a local slaughter plant, or purchase meat for freezing, the main thing is to make sure all equipment and preparation areas are kept clean. Wash all equipment including tables with hot, soapy water; then rinse several times with hot, clear water. Do this before you prepare meat for freezing and after.

One of the most common problems with home freezing of meat is that the freezer either doesn't have the capacity for quick freezing, or it may be so full of food that the capacity for fast freezing is reduced. If your freezer won't freeze the meat quickly at —10°F, the meat may deteriorate somewhat before it is solidly frozen.

If you slaughter the animal yourself, make sure the meat is thoroughly chilled before attempting to freeze it for storage. If all the animal heat isn't completely gone, it will result in poor quality meat with a bad odor and taste. The meat should be hung up and chilled quickly, somewhere between 33°F and 36°F within 24 hours of slaughtering. Pork and veal should be chilled for 1 to 2 days, lamb and beef for 5 to 7 days at these temperatures.

Cut and prepare meats for number of servings you will need to cook at one time. Wrap in two layers of paper—plastic wrap followed by freezer paper—and label each package with name, date, kind of meat, and number of servings.

Turning the freezer control to the coldest position will help in freezing the meat more quickly. Leave at this position for at least 24 hours before turning back to storage position. If you're only freezing a half freezer load or less, turn back after 12 hours. As with other frozen foods, you shouldn't freeze more than 2 pounds of fresh food per cubic foot of storage space in your freezer.

FREEZING PORK

Pork will not keep as well in the freezer as other meats. It should be used up within 8 months, or it will become rancid. Both fresh, cured, and smoked pork and prepared meats such as sausage may be frozen for storage, although cured pork will lose much of its flavor when frozen. Prepared meats such as sausage won't keep much more than a month or two before they start to lose flavor and become rancid tasting. The old-fashioned method of preparing sausage is to place in muslin bags and merely slice off the frozen patties as you desire. This is a very convenient method, but the meat won't stay fresh tasting as long because it will become dry more quickly. A more modern method is to make up the individual patties, separate them with sheets of waxed paper, place the number of servings desired in each package, and then wrap packages with two layers of paper. One thing to remember in preparing pork for freezing is to remove as much fat and bone as possible. When making up sausage, make sure you don't put in more than 1/4 fat.

Approximate trimmed pork cuts from a hog having a live weight of 225 pounds and a carcass weight of 176 pounds

Trimmed cuts	Yield (lbs.)	Live weight (%)	Carcass weight (%)
Fresh hams, shoulders, bacon, jowls	90	40	50
Loins, ribs, sausage	34	15	20
Total	124	55	70
Lard, rendered	12	15	27

FREEZING BEEF

Almost all beef will stay fresh tasting in the freezer for a year, except for liver and ground meat. Liver should be used up before 3 months, ground meat before 4 months. Prepare the meats for cooking by removing excess bone, fat, etc.; then place in double-wrap paper packages of family-size servings.

Make sure you keep the meat thoroughly chilled during preparation. Steaks, chops, etc., should be wrapped with a separating piece of waxed or freezer paper between them. Place ground meat in paper packages, about 1- to 2-pound sizes. Label, date, and freeze.

Approximate yields of trimmed beef cuts from animal having a live weight of 750 pounds and a carcass weight of 420 pounds

Trimmed cuts	Yield (lbs.)	Live weight (%)	Carcass weight (%)
Steaks and oven roasts	172	23	40
Pot roasts	83	11	20
Stew and ground meat	83	11	20
Total	338	45	80

Approximate yields of trimmed beef cuts from dressed forequarters weighing 218 pounds

Trimmed cuts	Yield (lbs.)	Weight of forequarters (%)
Steaks and oven roasts	55	25
Pot roasts	70	32
Stew and ground meat	59	37
Total	184	94

Approximate yields of trimmed beef cuts from dressed hindquarters weighing 202 pounds

Trimmed cuts	Yield (lbs.)	Weight of hindquarters (%)
Steaks and oven roasts	117	58
Stew, ground meat, and pot roasts	37	18
Total	154	76

WILD GAME, VENISON, RABBIT, SQUIRREL, ETC.

All these meats are prepared as beef, making sure as much fat and bone as possible is removed. Treat the slaughtering and preparation of meat as carefully and cleanly as you do beef or pork, and you will have good tasting meats, without the characteristic "wild flavor" often complained of in wild foods. Wild foods are somewhat drier than domestic meats, so they should be wrapped very carefully to prevent drying out and freezer burn, and they should be used up in 6 months.

Veal, lamb, and mutton are prepared in the same manner as beef.

Yields of trimmed lamb cuts from a lamb having a live weight of 85 pounds and a carcass weight of 41 pounds

Trimmed cuts	Yield (lbs.)	Live weight (%)	Carcass weight (%)
Legs, chops, shoulders	31	37	75
Breast and stew	7	8	15
Total	38	45	90

Storage Periods

The recommended storage periods for home-frozen meats and fish held at 0°F are given below. For best quality, use the shorter storage time.

Product	Storage period (months)	Product	Storage period (months)
Beef:		Pork, cured:[1]	
Ground meat	3 to 4	Bacon	1 month or less
Roasts	6 to 12	Ham	1 to 2
Steaks	6 to 12	Pork, fresh:	
Stew meat	3 to 4	Chops	3 to 4
Fish	6 to 9	Roasts	4 to 8
Lamb:		Sausage	1 to 2
Chops	6 to 9	Veal:	
Ground meat	3 to 4	Cutlets, chops	6 to 9
Roasts	6 to 9	Ground meat	3 to 4
Stew meat	3 to 4	Roasts	6 to 9
		Organ meats	3 to 4

[1]Frozen cured meat loses quality quickly and should be used as soon as possible.

POULTRY

Poultry for freezing may be grown and slaughtered on the farm or purchased at a market. Normally, birds purchased at a market are already cleaned, wrapped, chilled, etc. All you'll have to do is add more paper to prevent freezer burn or remove from package and disjoint or cut birds into pieces desired if you're not going to freeze them whole. Don't attempt to freeze the chickens in the same package in which they are displayed at the store. It isn't vapor- or moisture-proof. Make sure the birds are thoroughly wrapped, because poultry will freezer burn quite easily. If you are preparing fryers, cut up just as you would for table servings, placing the livers in a separate package. If you're packaging halves for barbecueing, etc., split the birds, place a double layer of freezer paper between the pieces, and then wrap tightly. If you slaughter your own poultry, make sure the carcasses are thoroughly chilled in a

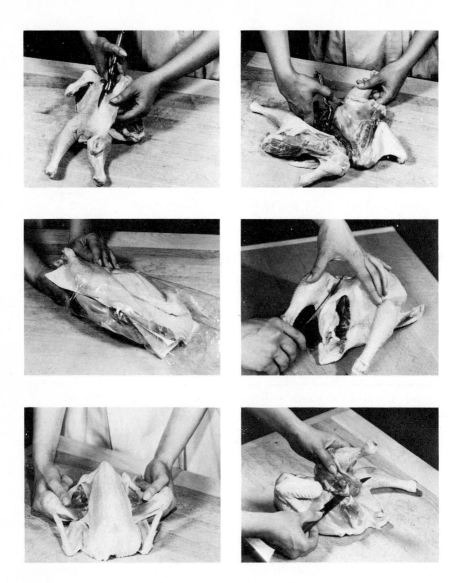

Top left, to prepare chicken halves for freezing, first remove neck and backbone by cutting along both sides of backbone. *Top right,* then cut in half along breastbone or remove breastbone and then cut in half. *Middle left,* place a double fold of freezer paper between chicken halves and wrap for freezing or place in plastic bags. *Middle right,* to prepare poultry for freezing, cut up bird by first cutting through the skin between leg and body. *Bottom left,* grasp legs and bend down until hip joints are free. *Bottom right,* then cut through that joint to remove leg and thigh from bird.

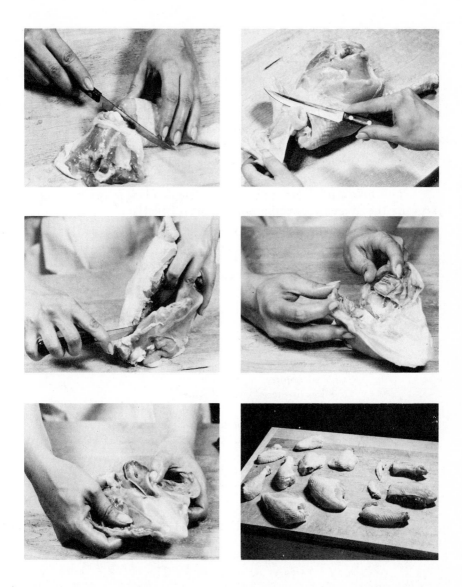

Top left, locate knee joint and cut through to separate leg and thigh. *Top right,* to remove wing, pull wing away from body and cut around joint. Pop joint and cut through. *Middle left,* to cut body cavity in half, stand bird up on neck edge and cut between legs. Then break back into two pieces. *Middle right,* to remove breast-bone, place breast skin side down on cutting board and cut through white cartilage at neck. *Bottom left,* grasp breast piece and bend back pushing up with fingers to snap out breastbone. Then cut breast meat in half. *Bottom right,* the pieces of a properly disjointed chicken.

refrigerator below 40°F for at least 12 hours before you place them in the freezer.

Turkeys and baking hens are wrapped and prepared in much the same manner as whole fryers. Poultry should be used in 3 months time.

Game birds such as quail, pheasant, duck, etc., should be frozen in the same manner as poultry; make sure you remove all traces of blood before freezing. Soak in salt water to remove congealed blood around wounds. Because the meat is dryer on these birds, make sure they are well protected by wrapping the packages properly, using two layers of paper. Use within 2 to 3 months.

The following chart indicates the length of time poultry can be kept in the freezer, providing the meat is good quality, is wrapped correctly, and a temperature of 0°F is kept.

	Months
Uncooked poultry:	
Chicken and turkey, whole	12
Chicken, cut up	9
Turkey, cut up	6
Duck and goose, whole	6
Giblets	3
Cooked poultry:	
Slices or pieces, covered with broth or gravy	6
Slices or pieces, not covered with broth or gravy	1
Cooked poultry dishes	2 to 6
Fried chicken	4

FREEZING FISH AND SHELLFISH

Fish may be frozen in a number of ways:

1. Whole—as they come from the water,
2. Drawn—entrails removed,
3. Dressed—normally the head, tail, fins, scales and entrails removed,
4. Steaks—slices made across the fish, normally from large specimens,
5. Fillets—slices made along the backbone to lift out a boneless section of meat.

Regardless of what method or kind of fish, make sure you wash and soak away all blood, slime, etc., before freezing. Some people allow the fish to cool in the refrigerator at below 40°F in water to which a bit of salt has been added. The fish is then prepared just as for cooking, wrapped, labeled, and frozen. You can also dip steaks and fillets into a 5% brine solution (2½ tablespoons salt to 1 quart water). Some folks like to place the fish in water in a used milk carton and freeze the fish in the carton, water-and-all, to prevent freezer burn. Make sure all fish is double-wrapped, first in vapor-proof freezer film, then in freezer paper.

Lobster, Fish Roe, Crab, and Oysters

All these are prepared just as you would use them fresh, washing thoroughly and then packaging in plastic freezer containers, leaving a bit of headspace. Label and freeze.

Shrimp

Shrimp may be prepared for freezing in one of several methods. They may be prepared by removing the head and freezing or by removing the head and shell, cleaning thoroughly, then freezing. In either method, the shrimp is packaged in plastic freezer containers. Cold ice water is poured over the shrimp before packaging, and a bit of headspace is allowed at the top of the container for expansion of the water.

Shrimp may also be prepared for serving by boiling for five minutes in saltwater (2½ ounces of salt to each gallon of water), then freezing.

Shrimp may be breaded before freezing by peeling raw shrimp, deveining, and breading with your favorite recipe. Place in freezer bags or double wrap freezer paper; label and freeze. Precooked shrimp may also be frozen in this manner.

FREEZING DAIRY PRODUCTS

Butter

Home-churned and fresh creamery butter will keep in the freezer 9 months if double-wrapped in moisture-proof packaging. Purchased butter should be rewrapped or placed in a tightly closed plastic bag before freezing. It's hard to know for sure how long purchased butter will keep in the freezer, since there is no way of knowing how fresh the product is; however, 6 to 7 months would probably be the longest.

Cheese

Most cheeses can be frozen; however, some freeze better than others. Some cheeses become crumbly after freezing, but they can still be used in cooked dishes. Cheese should be divided and packaged in small, one-serving packages. Double-wrap in freezer film and vapor-proof paper. They will keep approximately 6 months. Dry cottage cheese can be frozen for approximately one month. Pasteurized processed cheese should be left in the store container, adding a wrapping of vapor-proof paper. This will keep only 1 to 2 months. Soft cheeses generally don't freeze as well as hard cheeses.

Heavy Cream

Thick, heavy cream can be frozen and used in many dishes; however, it will not whip. To freeze, heat the cream to 180°F and hold for 15 minutes; add 1 tablespoon sugar to each cup of cream, and cool quickly. Package, leaving headspace, and label, date, and freeze. Storage time is 4 months.

Ice Cream

Homemade ice cream will keep in the freezer 6 weeks if packaged in vapor-proof containers. To serve, place in the refrigerator for 15 to 20 minutes before eating.

Purchased ice cream will keep about 3 weeks unless the store package is overwrapped with moisture-proof paper or placed in a tightly closed plastic bag. It will then keep 6 weeks.

After you've served from a carton of ice cream, crumple waxed paper into the empty space in the carton to exclude the air.

Whipped Cream

Place mounds of whipped cream on baking sheets and freeze. When frozen, pack into closed containers or plastic bags, and store about 1 month. To use, place frozen mounds on top of dessert servings, and serve immediately.

Eggs

Freeze only fresh, cleaned, shelled eggs. Break each egg into a dish and check for spots or spoilage before adding to other broken eggs.

To freeze whole eggs, stir gently with a fork to break yolks. Freeze in desired amounts in tightly closed, vapor-proof freezer containers.

Gently stir egg white and freeze in recipe amounts. Break yolk with fork and freeze in recipe amounts. Do not beat air into the eggs when mixing. Allow headspace in tightly closed containers. All eggs will keep for 8 to 12 months in the freezer.

To use frozen eggs:

3 tablespoons frozen mixed whole eggs = 1 whole egg
2 tablespoons frozen egg whites = 1 egg white
1 tablespoon frozen egg yolk = 1 egg yolk

Use defrosted frozen eggs quickly, as they will not keep over 24 hours.

Milk

Pasteurized milk may be frozen in plastic food containers or freezer jars. Leave about ¾ inch headspace. Frozen milk does not taste like fresh milk and is used only for cooking. The recommended storage time is 3 weeks.

3
JUICES

One of the best ways of preserving and using an excess of vegetables or fruits is in juices, and a frosty cold glass of tomato juice made from your own tomatoes and seasoned to your particular taste is indeed a great way to start a morning. Maybe you prefer pear juice, apple cider, or carrot juice. Or perhaps you would like to bottle your own fruit juices and "soft drink" to quench those thirsty kids in the summer. Regardless of what your thirst "flavor" is, you'll find that making your own fruit and vegetable juices is not only fun and truly economical, but a great way of becoming the "pride of the household."

EXTRACTING JUICE

When most of us think of juice, we think of tomato or orange juice; however, there are a lot of other fruit and vegetable juices that are just as good tasting and provide not only a nutritious way of enjoying these fruits and vegetables, but an unusual one as well. Raw vegetable juices have been a favorite with health-food fans for some time, but even if you're not particularly a health-food fan, you'll find this a great way of enjoying your home-grown vegetables.

For most vegetable drinks you'll need a "juicer." These are electrical appliances that separate the juice from the pulp in fruits and vegetables. The only problem is that these machines are rather expensive. Most of them will run $100 or more. The main purpose of these machines is to make fresh vegetable and fruit juices and once you've tasted cold

To prepare juice from any fresh fruits or vegetables, you will need a juicer such as the one shown.
(Courtesy of Acme Manufacturing Company)

APPROXIMATE NUTRITIONAL CONTENTS OF IMPORTANT JUICES

	BEET (Red)	CARROT	CELERY	CUCUMBER	LETTUCE Romaine	PARSLEY	RHUBARB	SPINACH	TOMATO	WATERCRESS	APPLE	COCONUT	GRAPE	GRAPEFRUIT	LEMON	ORANGE	PINEAPPLE	POMEGRANATE
PROTEIN %	1.6	1.1	1.1	0.8	1.2	3.5	0.6	2.1	0.9	1.7	0.1	1.4	1.3	0.4	0.9	0.6	0.4	1.5
FAT %	0.1	0.4	0.1	0.2	0.3	1.0	0.7	0.3	0.4	0.3	0.2	12.5	1.6	0.1	0.6	0.1	0.3	1.6
CARBOHYDRATE %	9.7	9.3	3.3	3.1	3.0	9.0	3.8	3.2	4.0	3.3	12.5	7.0	19.2	9.8	8.7	13.0	9.7	19.5
CALORIES PER PINT	220	217	89	84	94	283	115	115	112	109	250	700	462	200	210	265	207	472
CALCIUM %	0.140	0.225	0.390	0.050	0.345	0.350	0.220	0.390	0.055	0.785	0.035	0.120	0.055	0.105	0.110	0.120	0.040	0.030
MAGNESIUM %	0.130	0.100	0.140	0.045	0.065	0.160	0.085	0.250	0.065	0.170	0.040	0.100	0.045	0.045	0.045	0.055	0.050	0.020
POTASSIUM %	1.770	1.540	1.460	0.700	1.660	1.50	1.625	2.685	1.335	1.435	0.640	1.500	0.530	0.805	0.615	0.905	1.350	1.600
SODIUM %	0.485	0.385	0.645	0.050	0.100	0.200	0.125	0.445	0.060	0.495	0.055	0.180	0.025	0.020	0.030	0.060	0.080	0.250
PHOSPHORUS %	0.210	0.205	0.230	0.105	0.140	0.130	0.090	0.230	0.145	0.230	0.060	0.370	0.050	0.100	0.055	0.090	0.055	0.050
CHLORINE %	0.290	0.195	0.665	0.150	0.395	0.090	0.180	0.330	0.145	0.305	0.025	0.600	0.010	0.025	0.030	0.025	0.255	0.068
SULPHUR %	0.090	0.110	0.140	0.155	0.130	0.120	0.065	0.180	0.070	0.835	0.030	0.140	0.045	0.050	0.045	0.050	0.045	0.040
IRON %	0.004	0.003	0.003	0.002	0.007	0.016	0.003	0.013	0.002	0.015	0.002		0.0015	0.0014	0.003	0.002	0.002	0.004
SILICON %	0.009	0.007	0.008	0.013	0.018		0.006	0.020	0.009		0.006		0.002	0.002	0.0002	0.0007		
MANGANESE %	0.008	0.0005	0.0014	0.0013	0.0064	0.008	0.0013	0.0042	0.0012	0.0036	0.0003	0.0017	0.0001	0.0001	0.0002	0.0003	0.006	
COPPER %	0.001	0.007	0.001	0.016	0.0003	0.015	0.0005	0.001	0.0005	0.005	0.0008	0.0009	0.0005	0.0003		0.0008	0.0004	0.0005
IODINE Parts per billion.	230	180		500	650			400	350	180							200	120

This chart, prepared by the U.S. Department of Agriculture measures percentages of various nutritive elements in vegetable juices. The bulk of juice is of course water.

Cabbages eaten whole are 97 percent water, for instance, so by juicing them you are retaining more than 97 percent of their nutritive elements. August, 1972 fresh juice in this manner, you'll be hooked. The same machine, however, can be used to make juice from an excess of vegetables that you don't want to can or freeze. After extracting the juice, it's much easier and takes much less space to freeze the juice. Using these juicers, you can juice and freeze almost anything from carrots to beans, peas, spinach, celery, lettuce, Jerusalem artichokes, beets, etc.

The preceding chart gives the approximate nutritional contents of some of the most important juices.

Low-acid vegetable juices must be processed in a pressure canner to be processed properly. However, this results in a great loss of flavor and nutrition; therefore, vegetable juices are best frozen.

If you don't wish to invest in quite so expensive a juicer, you might be interested in a food mill similar to the one illustrated. Relatively inexpensive, this juicer will quickly juice tomatoes, berries, and other fruits and can be used to make such things as tomato paste and catsup, baby food, cream soups, apple sauce, fruit and vegetable purees, and many other things. We use it mostly for producing tomato puree, which can be used for tomato juice, tomato sauce, paste, taco sauce, catsup, etc.

To use in this manner, merely wash, remove stem ends of tomatoes, and cut into quarters. Then place in top hopper, and turn handle. Tomato puree will be separated from seeds, skins, and excess pulp. It isn't even necessary to peel the tomatoes, and they can be strained raw or simmered until soft, then strained.

Using the juicer shown, you can easily make purees and baby food. To prepare fruits, wash ripe fruit, remove pits, then cut into small pieces. Simmer until softened; then run through juicer to remove all skins, strings, etc. For vegetables, wash, remove stems, and cut into pieces; then

This food mill can be used to juice almost anything. Tomatoes and softer fruits can be juiced fresh. It will also make fresh applesauce. Just cut fresh apples in chunks and turn the crank.

Tomato juice can also be extracted by sieving the cooked tomatoes through a colander.

simmer until soft. Put through juicer, and you will have skinless, stringless vegetables. Freeze or dry the purees, or use in other recipes such as jams or butters.

Almost all pulp extracted with a food mill will have to be strained through a jelly bag to produce good clear juices for drinking or jellymaking. A muslin or cheesecloth bag and a colander or sieve can also be used to extract juice from soft or precooked fruits. These fruits can be forced through a colander or sieve with a pestle. For a clear juice for jelly or drinking, this pulp should then be drained through a jelly bag. Juice for drinking can simply be placed in the refrigerator overnight, then poured off, leaving the residue in the bottom of the bowl.

When reheating the strained fruit juices to 190°F before canning or freezing, heat the juice slowly in a double boiler arrangement to retain that fresh fruit taste. When adding sugar to the fruit juices, stir well until all sugar crystals have dissolved. Juice that is canned or frozen without sugar can be used for a wider variety of things. It can be cooked down later for fruit sodas, used to make jellies and gelatin desserts, or sweetened later for drinking.

Most fruits can be prepared in the same manner; however, some fruits are better if the juice is extracted from the raw fruit, and some are better if simmered first. The following recipes give further directions on how to prepare fruits.

FRUIT JUICES

Apple Juice

Probably one of the most popular and famous of fruit juices is apple juice, or apple cider. Apple cider was a very important beverage to the early Americans, and hard cider was consumed by everyone including women and children. The only difference between hard and sweet cider is that sweet cider is drunk fresh, pasteurized, or frozen so it will not ferment and is actually apple juice, while hard cider is cider that is allowed to ferment and age and may be stored indefinitely.

If you don't have an orchard with an excess of apples, you can still make apple cider much more economically than you can buy it. One good way to look for apples is during your hunting trips. Often you'll find abandoned farms or even old orchards where a farm homestead once existed. You can also take containers to many farms and orchards and pick your own apples at a greatly reduced cost. Depending on a lot of things—the efficiency of your press, the juiciness of the apples, etc.— it normally takes about a bushel of apples to make 2 to 3 gallons of cider. One of the great things about apple cider is that you don't have to have perfect apples. You can use apples that have dropped to the ground and are bruised or have slight blemishes, etc. Don't use wormy, decayed, or unripe apples, as you only stand the chance of tainting the flavor of the cider. It's a good idea to pick the apples and let them ripen for a couple of days before making them into cider.

Each type of apple also has a somewhat different flavor, and if you mix them up, you will have a better flavored cider. For instance Red Delicious, Baldwin, Cortland, Rome Beauty, Russet, Grimes, and Hubbardston are sweet apples. McIntosh, Golden Delicious, Ben Davis, Winter Banana, and Ribsten will add aroma. York Imperial, Winesap, Jonathan, Greening, Newtown Pippin, Wealthy, Northern Spy, and Stayman apples are somewhat tart tasting. Transcendent, Martha, Red Siberian, and Florence Hibernal are tangy.

Wash all the apples to remove any dirt or dust, and remove the stem and blossom ends. If the apples have been sprayed with pesticides, you should also wash them in a mild solution of muriatic acid (available at drug stores or hardware stores). The apples should be washed in a solution of 1 pint muriatic acid to 3 gallons of water. This solution is somewhat corrosive, so handle with care and *make sure you pour the acid into the water* and not the water into the acid. After washing apples in this solution, rinse them in clean water.

After cleaning thoroughly, the apples should be pulverized so they can be squeezed more easily. You can do this in a wooden barrel using a wooden stick or by running them through a food chopper, food mill, or even your garden shredder. However, it is best done by an apple mill that goes along with the apple press. These are often found at country auctions, although with the increasing interest in self-sufficiency, these and other old-time tools are selling at fairly high prices. The pomace should be as fine as you can get it, because you'll utilize more juice from the apples with finer pomace. Don't let pomace stand; start the pressing immediately.

For pressing you will need a cider press. With the growing popularity of cider-making, there are often old presses for sale, and many companies are now making them again, as well as kits that you can assemble yourself in order to save some money. Cider pressing is one of those jobs that takes patience and plenty of attention to detail. If you try to hurry the cider by squeezing the pomace too hard and too fast, you'll only end up with cloudy, inferior cider. Place a clean cheesecloth or muslin bag in the press and fill with pomace; then start turning down the press to squeeze the cider. Go slow, allowing the pomace to settle as you tighten the press down. It's also a good idea to fasten a couple layers of cheesecloth over the container catching the cider to further strain out any pomace or sediment. If the cloth becomes clogged, rinse it out in clear water or it will start releasing pomace and sediment into the sterilized juice. Cider may be squeezed off into almost any clean, sterilized glass or plastic bottles; however, most folks prefer the glass bottles, merely for the sake of appearance.

You'll often find that storage of cider isn't a problem because it goes so fast, but fresh sweet cider won't last much longer than a couple of weeks unless is it either frozen or pasteurized. Freezing is easy if you

A cider press can be used to press the juice from crushed apples for cider, but also can be used for grape juice, etc.

have the space; merely fill the containers (make sure they're either glass freezer containers, or plastic) up to about 90% full, and allow about 10% headroom for expansion. Cider will keep in your freezer for about a year.

You can also pasteurize the cider by heating it very quickly to 170°F in a stainless steel, aluminum, or other noncorrosive pan. Then immediately pour into sterilized containers or canning-type jars that can be closed airtight. After sealing the containers, place them in a tub of water which is about 165°F for five minutes, followed by placing them in lukewarm water for five minutes; then chill under cold running water.

You might wish to make hard cider, which was the cider kept in storage by the pioneers. To do this, you will need a wooden cider barrel or wine barrel. Wash it thoroughly with a bit of baking soda and warm water; then flush thoroughly with cold water. Fill with water, and allow the barrel to swell and soak for about a week before cider-making time.

Empty out the water, and place the barrel in a cool cellar, preferably a damp, dirt-floored cellar with a temperature of 50–55°F. Fill the barrel almost full through the bunghole in the top, and leave the bung out for three or four days. Add a bit of fresh cider each day. When the foam at the bunghole turns from dark brown to a light tan color, place a fermentation lock in the bunghole. One end of the fermentation lock is placed in a jar of water. When it stops bubbling from the end of the tube, the fermentation is complete. Remove the lock, place the bung in the bunghole, then pour hot paraffin around the bung to make sure you seal it properly in place. Allow the cider to age for about 6 months. It can be left indefinitely and drawn off as needed.

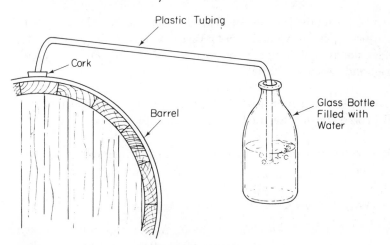

Fermentation lock for cider making.

Apple Vinegar

Vinegar is nothing more than apple cider that has been allowed to sour. After extracting the juice as in making cider, pour into a crock, and place in a basement or cellar that has a constant moderate temperature. Make sure it is covered with a cloth to keep out dirt and insects. It should be strong enough to use in about 3 to 4 months and should be stirred occasionally. Skim the scum off the top, bottle the vinegar, and store it in a cool, dark place.

Apricot Juice or Nectar

Wash firm, ripe apricots, and remove stems. Simmer whole fruits in water (2 cups water to 1 pound fruit) until tender; then press through sieve. Strain through cloth.

To Can: Heat juice to simmering (190°F), pour into hot sterilized jars, add lids, and process 10 minutes in boiling water bath.

To Freeze: Chill heated juice (190°F), and pour into freezer containers.

To Serve: Mix juice with equal parts of a thin syrup (1 cup sugar to 4 cups water), or mix with sugar and water to taste. Juice can also be mixed and sweetened before canning or freezing.

Berry Juices

(Blackberries, boysenberries, blueberries, elderberries, loganberries, raspberries, strawberries, or youngberries.) Wash berries, hull or stem, and crush. Heat slowly to 175°F, stirring to prevent sticking. Strain through a jelly bag, and sweeten to taste.

To Can: Heat strained juice to 190°F, pour into hot sterilized jars, add lids, and process 10 minutes in boiling water bath.

To Freeze: Heat strained juice to 190°F, chill in refrigerator, then pour into freezer containers.

Cherry Juice

Stem and pit cherries, then chop or mash. Add 1 cup water to each gallon of fruit. Heat to 170°F, stirring often. Press cherries through a sieve; then strain the juice. Sweeten to taste.

To Can: Heat strained juice to 190°F, pour into hot sterilized jars, add lids, and process 10 minutes in boiling water bath.

To Freeze: Heat strained juice to 190°F, chill in refrigerator, then pour into freezer containers.

Cranberry Juice

Boil cranberries with an equal amount of water until they burst. Strain through cheesecloth bag. Add sugar to taste, and heat to boiling.

To Can: Pour boiling juice into hot sterilized jars, add lids, and process 10 minutes in boiling water bath.

To Freeze: Chill juice in refrigerator, and pour into freezer containers.

Grape Juice

Stem and crush grapes. Add water if necessary—1 cup to 1 gallon grapes. Simmer until fruit is soft, but do not heat over 180°F. Press grapes through sieve. Leave juice in the refrigerator overnight to let crystals form and settle; then strain juice to remove crystals and sediment. Add sugar to taste—approximately 2 cups to 1 gallon juice—and heat to 190°F.

To Can: Pour hot juice into hot, sterilized jars, and process 10 minutes in a hot-water bath (190°F).

To Freeze: Chill hot juice; then pour into freezer containers.

Grapefruit Juice

Cut fruit in half and ream to extract juice, but do not press. Or fruit can be peeled, then pressed through a sieve. Strain juice and add sugar if desired.

To Freeze: Grapefruit juice is best reamed and frozen without adding sugar or heating.

Lemon or Lime Juice

Follow directions for Grapefruit Juice.

Orange Juice

Follow directions for Grapefruit Juice.

Peach Juice or Nectar

Follow directions for Apricot Juice.

Pineapple Juice

Peel and grind pineapple. Cover with water, and cook 15 minutes. Squeeze juice through jelly bag. Reheat juice to 190°F.

To Can: Pour hot juice into hot, sterilized jars, and process 10 minutes in boiling water bath.

To Freeze: Chill juice in refrigerator, and pour into freezer containers.

Plum Juice

Pit and crush plums. Add 1 cup water to each quart plums, and simmer until tender. Do not allow temperature to rise higher than 180°F. Squeeze juice through jelly bag, and add sugar to taste.

To Can: Reheat juice to 190°F, pour hot juice into hot, sterilized jars, and process 10 minutes in boiling water bath.

To Freeze: Chill juice, and pour into freezer containers.

Tomato Juice

Quarter fresh, ripe tomatoes, and remove stems. Mash slightly with a wooden spoon until juicy enough to cook. Simmer until soft. Press through a sieve or food mill, and measure. Add 1 teaspoon salt to each quart of juice. There is no need to strain tomato juice through a jelly bag.

To Can: Bring juice to boiling, pour into hot, sterilized jars, and process 10 minutes in boiling water bath.

To Freeze: Pour warm juice into freezer containers, cool, then freeze.

CATSUPS AND SAUCES

Blender Catsup

Follow the recipe for tomato catsup; however, don't cook and sieve the vegetables. Simply put the raw vegetables in your blender, and blend at high speed for a few seconds. Do not peel tomatoes first; the skins add significant nutrients to the catsup.

Oven or Slow-Cooker Catsup

Prepare tomato catsup. When it comes time to simmer the catsup until thick, merely put it in a 325°F oven, electric fry pan, or electric slow cooker. The catsup won't need the stirring and watching it would require if it were cooked on top of the stove.

Tomato Catsup

Bring to a boil 1½ cups vinegar, 1 cup sugar, 2 sticks cinnamon, 1 table-spoon whole cloves, 4 cloves garlic (chopped), 2 teaspoons celery seed, 1 teaspoon mustard seed, 1 teaspoon whole allspice, 1 tablespoon paprika, and 2 hot red peppers (chopped or crushed). Simmer 30 minutes; then cover, and remove from heat. Let stand until needed. Meanwhile, core about 6 quarts red tomatoes, and chop 1 cup onions and ½ cup sweet red peppers. Simmer until soft, and press through a food mill or sieve. Boil pulp until reduced in volume by half. Add 1 tablespoon salt and the strained vinegar solution. Cook to desired consistency, and process pint jars 10 minutes in boiling water bath.

Barbecue Sauce

    4 quarts red tomatoes, cored
    3 onions, quartered
    4 sweet red peppers, quartered
    2 hot red peppers, chopped

Combine, cook until tender, then press through food mill or sieve. Add: 2 cups brown sugar, 1 cup vinegar, 1 tablespoon dry mustard, 1 table-spoon paprika, 1 tablespoon salt, 4 cloves garlic crushed, 1 tablespoon Italian Seasoning, and a dash of Liquid Smoke (if available). Simmer to desired consistency, and process pint jars 20 minutes.

Chili Sauce

4 quarts red-ripe tomatoes, peeled, cored, and chopped
2 cups chopped onions
2 cups chopped green peppers
2 hot chili peppers chopped fine
3 cups brown sugar
3 cups chopped celery
3 tablespoons salt
2 teaspoons each: ground cloves, cinnamon, ginger, and nutmeg
1 cup white vinegar

Combine all ingredients, and boil rapidly until mixture thickens. Process pint jars 10 minutes in boiling water bath.

Taco Sauce

4 quarts red-ripe tomatoes, cored
3 cups chopped, hot red peppers
3 cups chopped onions
3 cups chopped celery
4 cloves garlic sliced

Combine the above ingredients. Put 2 to 3 cups at a time in your blender, and blend for a second at high speed. (Leave a few tiny pieces—you don't want taco sauce completely smooth.) Never fill blender over about half full. Continue until all the vegetables are pureed. Put the liquid into a large pan on the stove, and add the following: 1 cup brown sugar, 1 cup vinegar, 1 tablespoon salt, 1 tablespoon paprika, 2 teaspoons chili powder, 1 teaspoon Tabasco sauce, and 1 teaspoon allspice. Simmer to desired consistency. Taco sauce is usually much thinner than catsup. Process pint jars 15 minutes.

SYRUPS, TOPPINGS, AND SODAS

Berry Syrup

(Blackberry, raspberry, strawberry, boysenberry, blueberry, loganberry, dewberry, gooseberry, etc.) Mix 1½ cups sugar with each cup of berry juice, and bring to a full, rolling boil. Boil 1 minute. Remove from heat, and skim foam. Pour into hot, sterilized jars, and process 10 minutes in boiling water bath.

> *NOTE:* To test the consistency of the syrup, use the refrigerator test from Chapter 4 before canning the syrup.

Grape Syrup, Tame or Wild

Follow directions for Berry Syrup.

Berry Topping

Cook berries 5 minutes, mashing them as they cook. Add ¼ cup sugar for each cup of berries, and bring quickly to a hard, rolling boil. Boil until slightly thickened, pour into hot, sterilized jars, and process in boiling water bath 5 minutes. Again, use the refrigerator test before canning. Toppings should be slightly thick but not jelled as jams. You may wish to sieve some of the berries to remove some of the seeds.

> *NOTE:* A lot of different flavored syrups can be made by following the directions for jellies on your pectin packages, leaving out the pectin that jells the product. Also, undercooked no-pectin jellies can be processed and used as syrups. Jam recipes can also be used for other flavors of toppings by either undercooking no-pectin recipes or omitting the pectin from pectin recipes. Use the refrigerator test (Chapter 4) whenever making syrups to make sure you don't cook them long enough to jell. Remember, too, to use ripe fruit when making syrups, since you don't need the jelling power of the underripe fruits.

Fruit Sodas (Berries, Grapes, Oranges, Etc.)

Simmer strained fruit juice over a low heat until halved in volume. Add 1 cup sugar and 3 teaspoons cream of tartar to each cup of the concentrated juice, and stir well to dissolve sugar.

To Serve: Add approximately 1 ounce syrup and a pinch of bicarbonate of soda to an 8-ounce glass of water and ice. Stir and serve.

4
JAMS,
JELLIES,
AND PRESERVES

Homemade jams and jellies are probably the most elegant forms of food preservation. Other home-canned foods aren't always noticed, but homemade jams and jellies always bring a comment. Fruits preserved in this manner are simple, ready to be used in a number of ways, and require little in the way of canning equipment.

All you will need in the way of special equipment is a large (at least 8-quart) heavy-bottomed pan; a jelly bag (either a double layer of cheesecloth, muslin, or flannel); a colander and stand to hold the jelly bag; and a jelly, candy, or deep-fat thermometer to make some of the jams and jellies without pectin. A timer or clock with a second hand is also needed for the recipes using pectin.

Jelly can be preserved in almost any container; however, straight-sided jars are usually preferred because the jelly will slide out easily and can be served in an attractive mold. The decorative jelly jars on the market make attractive containers, especially for gift giving. These are all sealed with a thin, ⅛ inch layer of paraffin.

Jams, preserves, and other softer products are best preserved in pint or half-pint canning jars and are sealed with the two-piece metal lids. Fill jars, leaving ¼ inch headspace, with the hot liquid, and seal

Fill jars with hot jelly and leave ¼ inch headspace; seal immediately.

immediately. Prepare jar lids, and seal according to manufacturer's directions. Invert jars a few minutes; then turn upright to cool. If you are worried about your products keeping, particularly jams and preserves, they can be processed. A boiling water bath for 5 to 10 minutes should be sufficient for half-pint and pint jars.

Containers for your jellies and preserves should be prepared before you start cooking the jelly. Wash glasses and jars in hot soapy water, and rinse in hot water. Keep jars hot until you are almost ready to fill them. Either leave them in hot water or in a warm oven while preparing the jelly; then when almost ready to pour the jelly, invert the jars on a clean towel to allow the inside of the jars to drain dry before filling.

JAMS AND JELLIES
MADE WITH PECTIN

Jams and jellies made with liquid or powdered pectin are indeed the quickest and easiest to make. The cooking time is short, usually 1 minute at a full rolling boil, and the procedure is simple. Powdered pectin is mixed with the juice or fruit before heating, and liquid pectin is added to the boiling juice and sugar. However, the recipes and cooking times must be followed closely to insure a jelly of the proper consistency.

To make jam and jelly with pectin, you will, of course, have to purchase one of the pectin products on the market. Each brand contains specific recipes for making jellies with their product. If you are new to jelly-making and have formed no preferences, purchase at least one package of the products available in your area, and keep each recipe sheet as a guide to jelly-making. Some brands use more sugar than others, or the amount of fruit needed may vary, or the types of fruits covered may vary. Try all the brands at least once; then you'll probably find yourself continuing to use different ones for different fruits.

Below are a few additional recipes for jams and jellies using liquid and powdered pectin.

Red Cinnamon Apple Jelly

Add ¼ cup red cinnamon candy with the sugar to your favorite apple jelly recipe.

Top left, to prepare strawberry jelly with liquid pectin, first select and wash berries. *Top right*, remove stems from berries and crush. Line a colander with a clean, damp cloth, place this over a bowl and pour berries into cloth. *Middle left*, gather edges of cloth together and squeeze juice from berries. Strain juice again for a clear jelly. *Middle right*, measure juice and sugar into a large, heavy-bottomed pan and stir to dissolve sugar. Place pan over a high heat and stir constantly until mixture comes to a full boil. Add liquid pectin and let boil 1 minute. Remove from heat and skim. *Bottom left*, pour jelly immediately into hot jars leaving ½ inch headspace, then add a ⅛ inch layer of paraffin.

Top left, to make peach jam with powdered pectin, wash, peel and pit peaches. *Top right,* crush peaches. *Middle left,* measure peaches into a large, heavy-bottomed pan. *Middle right,* stir in powdered pectin and lemon juice, then place over a high heat and stir constantly until mixture reaches a full boil. *Bottom left,* add sugar all at once and continue stirring until mixture reaches a full boil. Boil 1 minute, remove from heat and skim. *Bottom right,* pour immediately into hot glasses leaving ½ inch headspace and adding ⅛ inch paraffin.

Cranberry Jelly

Follow the cooking instructions that come with your brand of powdered pectin using the following ingredients: 4 cups bottled cranberry juice cocktail, 1 package powdered pectin, and 5½ cups sugar.

Cranapple Jelly

Follow the above recipe using half cranberry juice and half apple juice. Or substitute half cranberry juice and follow the apple jelly recipe listed on your pectin.

Rose Geranium Jelly

Lay a clean, rose geranium leaf in the bottom of each jar just before filling with hot apple jelly.

Wild Grape Jelly

Cook according to the directions with the powdered pectin:

¼ cup lemon juice
6 cups wild grape juice
1 package powdered pectin
7½ cups sugar

NOTE: Do not try to stem the wild grapes. Simply wash them, and cut away the larger stem pieces. Simmer in water about 20 minutes; then strain juice for jelly.

Mint Jelly

Cover about 1 cup fresh, crushed mint leaves with about 3½ cups water, and bring to a boil. Remove from heat, and let stand 10 minutes. Prepare jelly according to powdered pectin instructions using 1 package powdered pectin to 3 cups strained mint liquid and 4 cups sugar.

Rhubarb Jelly

Grind rhubarb, and strain through bag. Mix together 4 cups rhubarb juice and 8 cups sugar. Bring mixture rapidly to a boil; then stir in 1 bottle liquid pectin. Bring to a full rolling boil, and boil hard 1 minute. Remove from heat, skim, fill jars, and seal.

Strawberry/Rhubarb Jelly

Extract juice as above using equal amounts each, or ⅔ strawberry to ⅓ rhubarb. To 4 cups mixed juice, use 7 cups sugar and 1 bottle liquid pectin, and proceed as above.

Blackberry/Blueberry Jam

Using the following ingredients, prepare according to the directions on the liquid pectin bottle:

> 3 quarts blackberries
> 1 pint blueberries
> 14 cups sugar
> 1 bottle liquid pectin

Blackberry/Huckleberry Jam

Substitute 1 pint huckleberries for the blueberries in the above recipe.

Blackberry/Plum Jam

Sieve blackberries to remove seeds; chop plums fine. Using the following ingredients, prepare according to the directions on the liquid pectin bottle:

> 9 cups mixed pulp
> 15 cups sugar
> 1 bottle liquid pectin

Blueberry/Raspberry Jam

Mash berries, strain if you wish to remove seeds, and measure using twice as much raspberry pulp as mashed blueberries. Prepare jam according to the recipe on the liquid pectin bottle.

> 4½ cups mixed fruit
> 7 cups sugar
> 1 bottle liquid pectin

Blueberry/Rhubarb Jam

Slice rhubarb in ½ inch pieces and crush blueberries. Use equal parts of each fruit. Prepare jam according to the recipe on the liquid pectin bottle.

   6 cups mixed fruit
   7 cups sugar
   1 bottle liquid pectin

Cherry/Plum Jam

Chop pitted red plums and cherries. Add ½ cup lemon juice to red plums, and simmer 5 minutes. Cook according to the directions on the powdered pectin package.

   6 cups mixed fruit
   8 cups sugar
   1 package powdered pectin

Cherry/Strawberry Jam

Using the following ingredients, prepare according to the directions on the liquid pectin bottle:

   4 cups chopped mixed fruit
   ¼ cup lemon juice
   7 cups sugar
   1 bottle liquid pectin

Peach/Pear Jam (Spicy)

Peel, pit, and core peaches and pears; then mash. Prepare according to directions with liquid pectin.

   4 cups mashed mixed fruit
   ¼ cup lemon juice
   7 cups sugar
   ½ teaspoon each ground cinnamon and nutmeg
   ½ bottle liquid pectin

Pear/Pineapple Jam

Peel, core, and chop pears. Prepare according to the directions with the powdered pectin.

   3 cups pears
   1 cup unsweetened crushed pineapple
   ¼ cup lemon juice
   1 package powdered pectin
   6 cups sugar

Raspberry/Rhubarb Jam

Slice rhubarb in ½ inch pieces, and cook until mushy—raspberries can be forced through a sieve if you wish to remove the seeds. Prepare according to the directions with the powdered pectin:

6 cups mixed fruit
8 cups sugar
1 package powdered pectin

Strawberry/Orange Jam

Prepare according to the directions with the powdered pectin.

4½ cups mashed strawberries
2 oranges (remove seeds and core; then grind)
1 package powdered pectin
6 cups sugar

UNCOOKED JAMS AND JELLIES

Uncooked jam and jelly recipes are a newer method of preserving your produce to keep that fresh-from-the-vine flavor. These are also called freezer jams, since they need to be stored in the freezer to preserve them. The fruit is not cooked in these recipes, just mixed with sugar, lemon juice, and pectin, and stirred. Powdered pectin is usually cooked in water first and then added to the fruit. Just remember to stir well to dissolve as many sugar crystals as possible so you won't have a sugary or gritty jam or jelly. The jam or jelly is then poured into containers, usually covered-plastic freezer containers or can-or-freeze jars, and allowed to set at room temperature. It may take up to 24 hours for the product to jell properly. Recipes for uncooked, freezer jams and jellies come with all the pectin products available, and the methods of preparing vary slightly with each.

JAMS, JELLIES, AND PRESERVES
MADE WITHOUT PECTIN

Making jams and jellies without the aid of commercial pectin requires time and a certain amount of knowledge and is indeed a real

Top left, to prepare the newer freezer or uncooked jams, stir sugar into prepared fresh fruits. Stir until sugar is dissolved and allow to set at least 10 minutes until sugar crystals disappear. *Top right,* stir in prepared pectin and continue stirring at least 3 minutes. *Side,* ladle into freezer containers and store in freezer.

old-fashioned art form. Our grandmothers learned through trial and error which fruits would jell properly. Today, however, we have pectin and acid tests which tell us whether or not the product will jell.

Pectin Test:

1. Cook 4 tablespoons juice and 2½ tablespoons sugar until thickened. If this mixture is jelled sufficiently when cooled, go ahead with your jelly-making.
2. Stir together I teaspoon juice and 3 teaspoons rubbing alcohol. *This mixture should not be tasted.* If this mixture forms a solid jelled mass, the juice is rich in pectin.
3. Stir together 2 teaspoons sugar, 3 teaspoons Epsom Salts, and 6 teaspoons fruit juice. Leave them for about 20 minutes. If this mixture forms a solid jelled mass, the juice is rich in pectin.

If the juice doesn't have enough pectin, it can be mixed with another juice that is high in pectin, or the fruit can be used to make jams or preserves. Cook and strain small amounts of fruit for juice to be used in the pectin tests.

To test the juice for acid, taste the juice. If it isn't as tart as 1 teaspoon lemon juice mixed with 3 tablespoons water and 2 teaspoons sugar, then lemon juice or citric acid should be added to the juice. Usually 1 tablespoon lemon juice or 1/8 teaspoon crystalline citric acid is added for each cup of juice.

The amount of sugar used in each recipe depends on the amount of pectin and acid in each fruit. Juices high in pectin usually require equal amounts of sugar and juice, while juices with a medium amount of pectin require only about 3/4 cup sugar to each cup of juice. Light corn syrup can replace up to one-quarter the amount of sugar called for in these recipes, and honey can replace up to one-half the amount of sugar.

To prepare fruits for jelly, wash and remove only stems and blossom ends. Do not peel, core, or pit. Hard fruits such as apples should be chopped and covered with water. Soft fruits and berries should be crushed adding only a little water. Cook until tender. Place a damp jelly bag in a stand or colander. Pour in the hot fruit, and let juice drain out. If you squeeze the bag to get all the juice, then you'll have to restrain the juice for clear jelly.

The safest way to know when your jelly is ready is to use a thermometer. A jelly, candy, or deep-fat thermometer will work. Determine the temperature of boiling water in your area, and add 8°F to it to find the correct temperature for your jelly to reach. This is called the "jellying point." For perfect jelly every time, make this test each day that you make jelly, as the humidity, etc., will change the temperature at which water will boil.

The next most reliable test is the *refrigerator test*. Pour a small amount of jelly in a flat plate, and place it in the refrigerator or freezer. If this jells in a few minutes, then the jelly is done. Remove the pan from the stove while conducting this test. This method works well for jams and preserves.

An old-time test for the jellying point is the *spoon test*. Repeatedly dip a metal spoon into the jelly; then lift it up out of the steam from the pan, and turn the spoon sideways to let the jelly run off. When the jelly quits dripping from the spoon and starts to thicken and pour off the spoon in a mass or sheet, you should be at the jellying point.

Remove the jelly from the heat, and let stand a minute until a film has formed. Remove this, or skim the jelly, and pour immediately into hot jars. To prevent floating fruit in jams, stir and skim for about 5 minutes before pouring into hot jars.

Below are some recipes for jellies, jams, preserves, conserves, marmalades, and butters. All are made without the addition of commercial pectin.

Apple Jelly

> 4 cups apple juice
> 3 cups sugar

Prepare juice by using ¼ underripe and ¾ fully ripe apples. Stir sugar into juice, and boil over a high heat until mixture reaches jelly stage. Remove from heat, skim, pour into jars, and seal.

Apple/Cinnamon Jelly

Add 1 drop oil of cinnamon to apple jelly just before pouring into jars.

Apple/Geranium Jelly

Add 1 cleaned rose geranium leaf to the bottom of each jar of apple jelly.

Apple/Mint Jelly

Add ¼ to ½ teaspoon peppermint extract to apple jelly just before pouring into jars.

Apple/Spiced Jelly

Make a cheesecloth bag containing a piece of stick cinnamon, a few whole cloves, and a few whole pieces of allspice. Add this to the apples while cooking them down for juice; then prepare as apple jelly.

Blackberry Jelly

Prepare juice using ¼ underripe and ¾ juicy ripe berries. Pour juice into a pan adding ¾ cup sugar for each cup of juice, and boil over high heat until the mixture reaches the jelly stage.

Crabapple Jelly

Remove blossom ends from crabapples; then quarter. Use approximately ¼ underripe and ¾ ripe fruit. Add water to barely cover fruit, simmer, and extract juice. Use 1 cup sugar for each cup of juice, and boil over high heat until mixture reaches the jelly stage.

Currant Jelly

Again use approximately ¼ underripe and ¾ ripe currants. Wash and sort, but do not remove from stems. Crush, add a little water, and simmer. Extract juice, and add 1 cup sugar for each cup juice. Boil over a high heat until mixture reaches the jelly stage.

Grape Jelly

Wash, sort, and stem ¼ underripe and ¾ ripe grapes. Crush, adding a small amount of water; then simmer until soft. Extract juice, and place in the refrigerator overnight. In the morning, strain the juice again to remove crystals, and proceed to make jelly using ¾ cup sugar for each cup of grape juice.

Peach Jelly

Peel peaches, cover with water, and simmer; then extract juice. Mix peach juice half and half with tart apple juice, and add 1 tablespoon lemon juice and ¾ cup sugar for each cup of mixed juice. Proceed to make jelly.

Pineapple Jelly

Simmer pineapple until tender; then squeeze out juice. Mix pineapple juice with equal parts tart apple juice. To each cup mixed juice, add ¾ cup sugar, and proceed to make jelly.

Plum Jelly

Again use ¼ underripe and ¾ ripe fruit. Cut fruit into pieces, but do not peel or pit. Simmer and extract juice. Add ¾ cup sugar for each cup of juice, and boil over high heat to the jelly stage.

Strawberry Jelly

Mix equal parts tart apple juice and strawberry juice. Add 2 teaspoons lemon juice and ¾ cup sugar for each cup juice.

Jams. Jams made without pectin are simply boiled until thick. No jelly test is necessary; however, the refrigerator test is useful in determining how thick the cooled product will be. If you wish to have your jams jelled to the same consistency every time, use a jelly, candy, or deep-fry thermometer, and boil to 9°F higher than the boiling point of water. Stirring and skimming jams for 5 minutes before filling jars prevents floating fruit.

> *NOTE:* Remember that jams stick easily and should be stirred constantly while cooking over high heat.

Apricot Jam

Peel, pit, and crush apricots. To each pint of crushed apricots add 1 tablespoon lemon juice. Mix crushed fruit with ¾ cup sugar for each cup of fruit, and cook over a high heat until thick.

Berry Jams

Add ¾ cup sugar to each cup crushed berries and juice, and boil until thick. This recipe will work for most berries and combinations of berries.

Blackberry Jam

4 cups crushed berries
4 cups sugar

Bring berries to a hard boil, and time for 2 minutes. Add sugar, stir until dissolved, and boil 1 minute. Beat hard for 4 or 5 minutes over a low flame.

Cherry (Mixed) Jam

Yellow sweet cherries
Red sweet cherries
Red sour cherries

Mix equal parts of pitted, chopped cherries. Add 1 cup sugar and 1 teaspoon lemon juice to each cup of fruit. Cook until thickened.

Cherry/Raspberry Jam

Mix equal parts of pitted sweet cherries, raspberries, and sugar. Cook to desired consistency.

Currant Jam

Simmer currants in a small amount of water until tender. Run through a food mill or sieve. Add 2 teaspoons lemon juice and ¾ cup sugar to each cup of pulp. Cook to desired consistency.

Currant/Blueberry Jam

Simmer blueberries in a small amount of water for about 5 minutes. Prepare currants as for the jam above, and mix blueberries with the currant pulp—approximately 2 cups blueberries to every 1 cup of currant pulp. Add 1 teaspoon lemon juice and ¾ cup sugar to each cup of fruit. Boil until thick.

Gooseberry Jam

Remove stems and blossom ends from ripe gooseberries, and grind. Add 1 cup sugar and 2 teaspoons lemon juice to each cup of berries. Cook until thickened.

Grape Jam

Pop skins from grapes. Simmer pulp until soft; then press through sieve. Chop skins and simmer until tender in a small amount of water. Mix the pulp and skins, and add 1 cup sugar to each cup of fruit. Cook until thickened.

Mulberry Jam

Use ¼ underripe and ¾ ripe berries. Stem berries, and let stand for 5 minutes in 4 tablespoons salt and 4 cups water. Rinse berries well, and drain. For each cup of crushed mulberries, add 1 tablespoon lemon juice and ¾ cup sugar. Cook until thickened.

Peach Jam

Peel and chop fully ripe peaches. Heat peaches slowly, adding no water until they soften. Crush and cook until tender. Add equal amounts of sugar, and cook until thickened over a high heat.

Peach/Apricot Jam

Combine equal parts peaches and apricots, and prepare as for peach jam.

Peach/Red Plum Jam

Combine fruits, and prepare as for peach jam. Pit plums, but do not peel; then chop fine.

Damson Plum Jam

> 4 quarts chopped damson plums
> 1 quart cold water

Simmer fruit in water until soft. Measure and add ⅔ cup sugar for each cup fruit. Stir over low heat until sugar is dissolved; then boil rapidly until mixture is thick and clear.

Strawberry Jam

Crush berries. Add 1 cup sugar to each cup of crushed berries, and cook until thickened.

Strawberry/Cherry Jam

Crush strawberries, and pit and chop cherries. Mix equal parts of fruit together, and add 1 teaspoon lemon juice and ¾ cup sugar for each cup of fruit. Cook until thickened.

Strawberry/Rhubarb Jam

Crush strawberries, and cut rhubarb into ½ inch pieces. Mix equal parts of fruits together, and proceed as with strawberry jam.

Preserves. Preserves are uniform pieces of fruit suspended in a thick syrup. This syrup can have the consistency of honey or it can be a semi-jelled form. Small, whole fruits are the most attractive for preserves; however, uniform pieces of larger fruits are quite often used. To keep fruit pieces plump in the syrup, let softer fruits stand in sugar until their juices flow. Harder fruits should be precooked in a small amount of water before the sugar is added. Pouring the warm preserves into a shallow pan to cool is another method of plumping the fruit. The preserves should then be sealed in jars and processed in a boiling water bath—5 minutes for half-pints, and 10 minutes for pints. Honey or white corn syrup can replace any or all of the sugar in preserve recipes. Substitute either, cup for cup, with sugar. Preserves are cooked until thick or until a temperature of 9°F above the boiling point of water is reached. Stirring and skimming preserves for at least 5 minutes before pouring into jars helps prevent floating fruit.

Apple Preserves

Bring to a boil 2 cups sugar and 1 cup water. Stir constantly until this mixture reaches the hard ball stage. Add 1 quart thinly sliced peeled apples and simmer until apples are tender and transparent. Seal.

Apricot Preserves

Mix together 5 cups of halved, peeled apricots, 4 tablespoons lemon juice, and 4 cups sugar. Cover, and leave in refrigerator overnight. Heat slowly to a boil, stirring until sugar is dissolved. Boil rapidly until mixture thickens and apricots are transparent.

Cantaloupe Preserves

Peel a 2-pound ripe cantaloupe, remove seeds and strings, and cut in thin 1 inch slices. Mix with 4 cups sugar and 2 tablespoons lemon juice, and place in refrigerator overnight. Cook mixture to desired consistency.

Cherry Preserves

    5 cups pitted sour cherries
    4 cups sugar

Drain juice from cherries and dissolve sugar in juice (add water if necessary). Simmer until sugar is dissolved. Allow the syrup to cool; then add cherries, and boil rapidly to the desired consistency or until cherries are glossy and syrup thickens.

Grape Preserves

Halve grapes, and remove seeds. Combine with equal amounts of sugar, and cook to desired consistency.

Peach Preserves

Simmer 9 cups of sliced, underripe peaches in 1 cup water until just tender. Drain liquid, and dissolve 6 cups sugar in the liquid. Boil this syrup until it spins a thread; then add peaches, and boil rapidly for 10 minutes. Remove from heat, and skim. Pour into shallow pans, and let stand 24 hours. Pack and seal, or reheat and then pack and seal.

Pear Preserves

Simmer 3 quarts of sliced or chopped pears in 3 cups of water until tender; then drain. Stir 4½ cups sugar into drained liquid; then add pears when partially cooled. Boil rapidly until pears are transparent. Pour into shallow pans to cool; then reheat to boiling, pack, and seal.

Damson Plum Preserves

    2 quarts pitted plums
    6 cups sugar

Pour sugar over fruit, and let stand 3 or 4 hours. Cook rapidly until liquid reaches the jellying stage.

Red Plum Preserves

Combine 8 cups pitted red plums, 6 cups sugar, and 1 cup water. Heat slowly until sugar is dissolved; then boil rapidly until syrup reaches the jelly stage.

Strawberry Preserves

Mix equal parts of fruit and sugar, and cook for 3 minutes. Add half the amount of sugar again, and cook 3 more minutes. Pour out into shallow pans, and let set for 3 days, stirring every morning. Heat to simmering, and pack hot.

   NOTE: This recipe works well with cherries, pears, or peaches.

Tomato Preserves

Scald, peel, and quarter 5 pounds ripe red, yellow, or green tomatoes (about 12 cups). Add 4 pounds sugar, and place in the refrigerator overnight. Drain off juice, and boil rapidly until the juice spins a thread. Add tomatoes and 2 thinly sliced lemons (seeds removed), and boil until thick and clear.

Watermelon Rind Preserves

To prepare rind, remove all green skin and pink flesh, and cut white portion into 1 inch cubes. Cover with a mild salt solution (2 tablespoons salt to 1 quart water), and leave overnight. Drain and rinse well. Cook in clear water until fork tender. For 12 cups of rind, make a syrup of 9 cups sugar, 8 cups water, 4 lemons thinly sliced (seeds removed), and a bag containing 4 teaspoons broken-up stick cinnamon and 4 teaspoons whole cloves. Bring syrup to a boil and cook 5 minutes; then add rind and cook until transparent. Remove spice bag, pour, and seal.

Conserves and Marmalades. Conserves are mixtures of fruits and usually have nut meats and raisins added. Marmalades are fruit combinations with the addition of citrus fruits or are made from citrus fruits alone. Conserves and marmalades are cooked to the same consistency as jams and preserves, until fruit is transparent, syrup is thickened, or to 9°F above the boiling point of water.

Apple Conserve

    1 quart peeled, chopped apples
    3 cups sugar
    2 cups raisins
    1 orange peel sliced thin
    2 oranges, juiced
    1 lemon peel sliced thin
    1 lemon, juiced

Combine all ingredients. Cook slowly to desired consistency, stirring occasionally. Add ½ cup chopped nuts during the last 5 minutes of cooking.

   NOTE: For sweet apples, reduce sugar to 2 cups.

Apple/Blueberry Conserve

    4 cups peeled diced apples
    4 cups blueberries
    ½ cup seedless raisins
    4 tablespoons lemon juice
    6 cups sugar

Combine ingredients. Bring slowly to a boil, and stir until sugar is dissolved; then boil rapidly to desired consistency. Add ½ cup chopped nuts during the last 5 minutes of cooking.

Apple/Cherry Conserve

    4 cups pitted cherries
    2 cups pared, chopped apples
    1 cup chopped pineapple
    5½ cups sugar

Combine ingredients. Let stand a few hours or until juices flow. Cook slowly until all sugar is dissolved; then cook rapidly to desired consistency. Add ½ cup chopped nuts and 4 tablespoons lemon juice during the last 5 minutes of cooking time.

Apricot/Almond Conserve

    12 cups peeled, diced apricots
    3 oranges, diced (seeds removed)
    3 orange peels, ground
    ½ cup blanched almonds, ground
    10 cups sugar

Combine ingredients. Cook rapidly to desired consistency, stirring often.

Apricot/Orange Conserve

    10 cups chopped, peeled apricots
    1½ cups orange juice (seeds removed)
    4 teaspoons grated orange peel
    3 oranges, peeled, then diced (seeds removed)
    1 lemon, juiced

Combine ingredients. Boil rapidly to desired consistency. Add 1 cup chopped nut meats the last 5 minutes of cooking.

Blueberry/Pineapple Conserve

Combine 2 parts blueberries and 1 part finely chopped pineapple. Add ¾ cup sugar for each cup of fruit, and heat slowly to a boil, stirring until sugar is dissolved. Boil rapidly to desired consistency. Add nut meats if desired.

Cantaloupe/Peach Conserve

Combine equal parts peeled chopped cantaloupe and peeled chopped peaches. Simmer slowly until juicy, adding no water. Add ¾ cup sugar and 1 tablespoon lemon juice for each cup of fruit, and boil until thick. To each 4 cups of fruit add ¼ teaspoon ground nutmeg, a pinch of salt, ½ teaspoon grated lemon or orange peel, and ½ cup chopped nut meats. Cook about 5 minutes more.

Cherry/Raspberry Conserve

Simmer pitted sweet cherries until tender. Add equal amounts of raspberry pulp and ⅔ cup sugar for each cup of fruit. Cook rapidly to desired consistency, adding nut meats if desired.

Cranberry/Orange Conserve

      2 orange peels, thinly sliced
      2 oranges, peeled and diced (seeds removed)
      2 quarts cranberries
      2 cups raisins
      1 cup chopped nut meats
      6 cups sugar

Combine orange peels, cranberries, and raisins and about 2 cups of water. Simmer until tender. Add orange pulp and sugar, and cook to desired consistency. Add nuts during the last 5 minutes of cooking time.

Gooseberry Conserve

Combine 2 quarts stemmed gooseberries, 1 unpeeled orange finely chopped, 1 cup raisins, and 4 cups sugar. Bring to a boil slowly, stirring to dissolve sugar. Boil rapidly to desired consistency, stirring often. Add ½ cup chopped walnuts or almonds, and cook an additional 5 minutes.

Gooseberry/Rhubarb Conserve

Mix stemmed gooseberries and diced rhubarb. Add ¾ cup sugar for each cup of fruit, and cook to desired consistency. Add nut meats during the last 5 minutes of cooking time.

Grape Conserve

Slip skins from 2 quarts stemmed grapes. Place the skins in a large kettle with about ¼ cup water, and simmer until tender. Place the pulp in another kettle, and simmer until tender. Press pulp through a sieve to remove seeds. Combine skins and pulp, and add 2 oranges chopped fine (seeds removed), 1 cup raisins, and 6 cups sugar. Cook to desired consistency, and add 1 cup chopped nuts and a dash of salt.

Apple Marmalade

    2 quarts pared, thinly sliced apples
    1 orange quartered and thinly sliced (seeds removed)
    1 lemon quartered and thinly sliced (seeds removed)
    1½ cups water
    5 cups sugar

Dissolve sugar in water, and add fruit. Boil rapidly to jellying stage. Remove from heat, and skim and stir before sealing.

Apricot Marmalade

Peel, pit, and dice apricots. Simmer in a small amount of water until tender. Press apricots through a sieve and measure. Bring pulp to a boil, and add equal amounts of sugar, stirring until sugar is dissolved; then boil rapidly until thickened. Since apricots will scorch easily, they should be stirred and watched constantly.

> *NOTE:* Spices, nuts, and/or citrus peels may be added to this recipe.

Sweet Cherry Marmalade

    2 orange peels, finely diced
    2 oranges diced (seeds removed)
    6½ cups sugar
    2 quarts pitted sweet cherries
    1 lemon peel, finely diced
    2 lemons, juiced

Cover peels with water and simmer until tender. Allow the peels to cool; then add oranges, cherries, and sugar. Cook slowly until sugar is dissolved; then boil rapidly to desired consistency.

Citrus (Mixed) Marmalade

Remove the peels from 1 grapefruit, 4 oranges, and 1 lemon. Thinly slice the peel, and cut in 1 inch pieces. Cover peel with cold water, bring to a boil, and let stand in refrigerator overnight. Drain and discard liquid. Add 1 quart cold water, and cook until tender. Add the chopped pulp from the grapefruit, oranges, and lemon. Measure fruit and liquid, and add 1 cup sugar for each cup. Cook to desired consistency.

Grapefruit Marmalade

Remove the skins from 3 large grapefruit. Remove the white part of the skin, and slice the rest in thin, 1 inch pieces. Cover the peels with cold water, and simmer until tender. Drain and discard liquid. Remove seeds and membrane from fruit, and dice. Mix together fruit, peel, and 2 quarts water. Bring to a boil; then add 1 cup of sugar for each cup of fruit and water. Boil rapidly to desired consistency.

Lemon Marmalade

Cover 1 cup thinly sliced lemons with 3 cups water, and cook until tender. Drain and measure liquid; add water to bring liquid back to 3 cups. Combine with 2 cups sugar, and boil rapidly to the desired consistency.

Orange Marmalade

Thinly slice 6 large oranges and 2 lemons; remove seeds and core. Mix fruit with about 2 quarts water, and bring just to boiling. Cover, and let stand overnight. Simmer fruit until tender; then add 1 cup sugar for each cup of fruit and juice. Cook to desired consistency.

Orange/Lemon Marmalade

Make as above for orange marmalade using half oranges and half lemons.

Orange/Peach Marmalade

  12 peaches pitted and peeled*
  3 oranges (seeds and core removed)

Grind peaches and oranges, and add 2 tablespoons lemon juice. Measure, and add 1 cup sugar for each cup fruit. Cook slowly, stirring until sugar is dissolved. Then cook rapidly to desired consistency.

Orange/Pineapple Marmalade

Thinly slice 6 oranges and 1 lemon, remove seeds and core. Cover with water, and simmer until tender. Let stand in refrigerator overnight. Add 5 cups chopped pineapple, and then measure. Add 1 cup sugar for each cup of fruit and juice. Cook to desired consistency.

Pear/Pineapple Marmalade

    2 cups orange pulp
    9 cups ground pears
    2 cups finely chopped or crushed pineapple
    ¼ cup lemon juice
    ½ cup maraschino cherries, thinly sliced

Remove seeds and core from oranges and peels and core from pears. Grind; then add pineapple and lemon juice. Measure and add ½ cup sugar for each cup fruit. Cook to desired consistency, and add cherries during last 5 minutes of cooking time.

Fruit Butters and Honeys. Fruit butters are simply fruit pulp thickened and sweetened. Sugar is usually added at the rate of ½ cup to each cup of fruit pulp, so they are not as sweet as jams or preserves. Fruit butters can be made plain or spiced, or mix some of your favorite fruits together for a really different butter. After straining juice for jelly, the pulp can be run through a food mill or sieve and used for butter.

As the butters cook down and get thick, they will stick and scorch easily and also do a great deal of sputtering. Lower the temperature as much as possible, using an asbestos mat under the kettle if your burners won't adjust low enough. For easier cooking and less pot-watching, try cooking down the butters in a moderate oven (a large roaster works well for this), or try one of the newer slow cookers. Containers should be uncovered so that the steam can escape. Stir occasionally to keep a film from forming on top of the butter.

The test for butters is the same as for jams and preserves: $-9°F$ above the temperature of boiling water. Another test is to pour a spoonful of butter on a chilled plate. If a water ring forms around the butter, it needs to cook longer. Butters can be sealed with paraffin or processed in a boiling water bath for 5 minutes.

Apple Butter (Spiced)

>   4 quarts apple pulp
>   8 cups sugar
>   4 teaspoons cinnamon

Core and slice apples, but do not peel. Add 1 cup vinegar or apple cider to the apple slices, and cook until tender. You may have to add more water if this is not enough liquid for the apples. Run apples through a food mill or sieve. Combine with above ingredients, and cook to desired consistency.

Apple/Lemon Butter

>   4 quarts apple pulp
>   8 cups sugar
>   4 teaspoons grated lemon peel

Prepare apples as above, and cook in ½ cup lemon juice and ½ cup water. Add more water if necessary. Complete as above.

Apricot Butter

Pit apricots, and mash until juicy. Simmer until tender. Press through a sieve or food mill. Add ½ cup sugar (or to taste) to each cup pulp. Cook to desired consistency.

>   NOTE: Apricots can be cooked in orange juice or lemon juice
>   and water with orange or lemon peel added for flavoring.
>   Or cinnamon and nutmeg may be added for a spiced
>   version.

Crabapple Butter

Quarter crabapples, and cover with water. Simmer until tender, and press through sieve or food mill. Add ¾ cup sugar for each cup of pulp, and cook to desired consistency. Cinnamon and nutmeg can be added for a spiced butter (about ⅛ teaspoon per pint of pulp).

Grape Butter

Mash whole grapes, and cook until tender, adding no water. Press through food mill or sieve. Measure, adding ½ cup sugar for each cup of pulp. Cook to desired consistency.

> NOTE: Cinnamon, nutmeg, or lemon can also be added to the grape butter.

Peach Butter

Scald, peel, and pit peaches. Mash peaches until juicy, and cook until tender. Add water if necessary. Press through sieve or food mill, and add ½ cup sugar for each cup pulp. Cook to desired consistency.

> NOTE: Peach butter is good plain or with nutmeg, cinnamon, and/or ginger.

Pear Butter

Wash, core, and cut pears into chunks. Mash until juicy, and cook until tender. Press through sieve or food mill, and add ½ cup sugar to each cup pulp. Cook to desired consistency.

> NOTE: Cinnamon and/or nutmeg may be added for spices or grated orange rind for flavor.

Plum Butter

Wash, pit, and mash plums. Simmer until tender. Press through sieve or food mill. If pulp is too watery, drain off some of the liquid before cooking. Add ½ cup sugar for each cup of pulp, and cook to desired consistency. Spices may also be added to plum butter.

Rhubarb Butter

Slice rhubarb into small pieces, and puree in blender. Add a small amount of water if necessary. Add ¾ to 1 cup sugar to each cup of pulp, and cook to desired consistency.

Strawberry/Rhubarb Butter

Prepare as for rhubarb butter using about half strawberries. Reduce sugar to not more than ¾ cup to each cup pulp. If you mix rhubarb and strawberries together to blend, you shouldn't have to add extra water.

> *NOTE:* Other fruits that have been peeled and pitted or cored can be prepared for butters in the blender. Plums are even good blended with the skins on. Your butter will be more fibrous, but you will also have more volume and nutrition from your fruit.

Lemon/Pear Honey

Follow pear honey recipe adding the juice and grated peel of one lemon.

Lime/Pear Honey

Follow pear honey recipe adding the juice and grated peel of one lime.

Orange/Pear Honey

Follow recipe for pear honey adding the juice and grated peel from one small orange.

Peach Honey

8 cups ground peaches
1 orange, ground

Peel and pit peaches, and remove seeds and core from orange; then grind. Add ⅔ cup sugar for each cup fruit, and cook to desired consistency.

Pear Honey

2 quarts ground pears
2 cups ground or crushed pineapple
5 cups sugar

Peel and core pears; then grind. Mix with pineapple and sugar, and cook to desired consistency.

5
PICKLES
AND RELISHES

Pickling is a favorite, old-time way of preserving food. Brined or fermented pickles were the earliest form of this well-known art and involved a fairly long process. Today, however, there are many short-cut recipes or "make-in-the-jar pickles." When you think of pickling, don't stop with cucumbers—they're only the beginning. Years ago, many different fruits and vegetables were preserved throughout the winter in crocks filled with a brining solution and stored in the root cellar. Eggs and cheese were also preserved in a brine. Sauerkraut is probably the best known brined vegetable; however, beans, turnips, cauliflower, carrots, corn, and even green tomatoes can be brined.

Relishes were also once a brined product. Today, however, most recipes are faster and are canned rather than brined. It is recommended that all pickled products be packed in jars and processed in water-bath canners after the brining process. Processing time is given with each recipe; however, if you are adapting an old recipe, a simple rule-of-thumb is 5 minutes for pints and half-pints and 20 minutes for quarts, or follow a recipe with similar ingredients. When processing dill pickles, start counting processing time as soon as the jars are placed in the boiling water and the canner is covered. Don't wait for the water to resume boiling to start timing. However, the less-acid sweet pickles shouldn't be timed until the water has returned to a boil.

EQUIPMENT

Crocks. For brining pickles and kraut, you will need crocks, enamel-lined pans, or large glass containers. You will also have to have glass plates or paraffined wooden lids that fit just down inside these containers, as well as cleanable weights (a glass jar filled with water) to hold the vegetables down in the brine. A 2-gallon, straight-sided crock is a good size for pickle recipes that require changing the brine once or twice a day. Larger crocks are difficult to handle but are needed for making kraut.

Pans. Stainless steel, glass, aluminum, or enamel-lined pans are needed to heat the brining solution.

Some of the equipment needed
to make pickles and relishes.

Jars. Clean, unchipped glass canning jars and new sealable lids. (Follow manufacturer's instructions for sealing lids.)

Canner. If you don't have a regular water-bath canner, your pressure canner can be used; just leave the vent open, and set the lid in place. Do not tighten lid. If you have neither of these, any pan that meets the following requirements may be used: One that is tall enough to cover the jars with 1 to 2 inches of boiling water and another 1 to 2 inches of boiling room; and one that has a close-fitting lid and a wood or metal rack of some sort to keep the jars up off the bottom of the pan.

Grinder. A hand-operated or electric food grinder is essential in making large quantities of relishes and chutneys.

Scales. Household scales are needed for weighing exact amounts of ingredients for sauerkraut and pickle recipes.

Miscellaneous. Along with the above items, there are several other items that will be needed: A jar lifter, wooden or stainless steel stirring spoons, measuring cups and spoons, a colander or strainer, a jar funnel, paring and slicing knives, and a cutting board.

INGREDIENTS

Fruits and Vegetables. Use only freshly picked fruits and vegetables for pickling and brining. Pick or purchase only as much at one time as you can put up or get into a brine that morning or day. Small, freshly picked batches are much better tasting and a lot less work and worry. Wash all fruits and vegetables in cold water until all dirt and debris is removed. Handle everything tenderly to avoid bruising. Make sure the blossoms are removed from all cucumbers. If purchasing cucumbers to be preserved whole, be sure they haven't been waxed. Brining will not penetrate a wax coating.

Salt. Use regular canning and pickling salt for best results. If this is not available, un-iodized table salt can be used. Iodized table salt will darken pickles, while table salt makes a cloudy brine.

Vinegar. Use only high-quality, 4% to 6% acidity, distilled vinegar. Do not use vinegar that doesn't have the acidity content on the label. Cider vinegar is used for most pickling; however, white vinegar can be used for any product that is to remain light in color, such as onions, cauliflower, and some fruits. Do not change the amount of vinegar called for in a recipe. If you wish to change the taste a bit, adjust the amount of sugar called for.

Sugar. Either granulated white or brown sugar can be used in pickling. White granulated sugar is used in most recipes for clear, light-colored pickles. However, some recipes call specifically for brown sugar.

Spices. This covers everything from the mixed pickling spices purchased prepackaged and ready-to-use to peppers, garlic, and grape leaves. The purchased, mixed spices should be bought fresh for each pickling season, and these are used in most recipes. Garlic should be fresh from the garden or purchased. Hot peppers can be purchased crushed and dried in cans, or use those fresh from the garden. Dill seeds and weed can be used fresh from the garden. They are also usually available fresh in supermarkets during the pickling season. Alum, which is used in many pickle recipes for crispness, is not needed if grape leaves or green grapes are added to the pickles. Turmeric is added for color. Mustard seed, celery seed, cinnamon sticks, and whole cloves are all available from the grocer. These should also be purchased fresh for each pickling season.

BRINED PICKLES

These pickles include all the old-fashioned, long-process pickles that were considered one of the staples before canning and freezing came into being. They were made in large crocks in the cellars and often left in these crocks until used. Of course, the coolness of the cellar helped in keeping the pickles, but any that didn't keep were just skimmed off and thrown away. Occasionally the pickles were put up in smaller crocks, and these smaller containers were covered with paraffin. These pickles take anywhere from 3 to 14 days to prepare. And yes, they are worth the effort.

Always wash and scald your crock before starting a batch of pickles. Brined pickles need to be checked daily, and any accumulation of scum removed. You might also wish to rewash and scald the crock at the end of, say, a week-long soak in a saltwater brine.

Always weight down pickles to hold them in the brine. Any pickles out of the brine won't keep. Do this by placing a clean, scalded glass plate or pie plate over the pickles and by weighting this down with a clean, glass jar filled with water. A polyethylene bag partially filled with water will serve both purposes. Make sure you use a sturdy bag with no holes.

Brined Dills

In the bottom of a clean, 5-gallon crock, place ½ cup whole mixed pickling spices and a layer of dill weed. Fill with cleaned, whole cucumbers to within 4 or 5 inches from the top. Be sure the cucumbers are a size that will later fit in your jars. Sprinkle another ½ cup of spices and another layer of dill weed on top. Thoroughly mix enough brine to cover the cucumbers using these proportions: 1 cup salt to 1½ cups vinegar to 1½ gallons water. Cover cucumbers with a glass plate and a weight as mentioned earlier; then cover loosely with a clean cloth. Check daily, and remove scum as it forms. If brine drops below level of pickles, make more brine using same proportions, and add to crock.

Pickles should have a good color and flavor in about 3 weeks. Pack pickles in clean, hot jars along with a sprig of dill and a clove of garlic. Strain brine and bring to boiling; then cover pickles with boiling brine. Adjust lids, and process in boiling water bath for 15 minutes.

Cinnamon Rings

Remove seeds from ½ inch slices of cucumber, and place in a crock. (Use the following proportions for each gallon of cucumber slices.) Cover slices with 1 cup salt and 1 gallon of water. Cover, and leave one week. Drain. Simmer for 2 hours ½ cup vinegar, 1 teaspoon alum, ½ teaspoon red food coloring, the cucumber slices, and enough water to cover. Drain.

Top left, place a layer of dill and spices in the bottom of a large crock, then fill crock with cucumbers. Place a layer of dill and spices over the top, prepare the pickling brine and cover the cucumbers with the liquid. *Top right,* place a weight over the pickles to make sure all stay under the brine. *Bottom left,* remove pickles from brine and strain brine through a cloth. *Bottom right,* pack pickles into hot jars and cover with boling brine leaving ½ inch headspace. Process 15 minutes in boiling water bath. Then remove jars from canner and set on rack to cool.

Bring to boiling a syrup of 6 cups sugar, 3 cups vinegar, 1 cup water, and 2 sticks of cinnamon (broken up). Pour over pickle slices, and let stand 12 hours. Drain, reheat, and pour over slices. Repeat this for 3 more days. Pack as usual, and process for 5 minutes for pints in boiling water bath.

Petite Pickles

Fill a crock with cleaned 2- to 3-inch cucumbers. Cover with boiling water, weight, and cover. Leave overnight and drain. Cover with fresh boiling water for the next 5 days. Drain. Cover pickles with a brine of 1 gallon water to 3 tablespoons salt. Leave overnight; then drain. Pierce each pickle, or cut a bit off one end so the sugar and vinegar can be absorbed throughout.

Bring to a boil enough syrup of the following proportions to cover the pickles: 1 quart vinegar to 1 cup water to 4 pounds sugar to 4 table-spoons mixed pickling spices. Pour hot over pickles, cover, and leave overnight. Fill jars as usual, and process for 10 minutes for pints in boiling water bath.

Ripe Cucumber Pickles

Peel, seed, and cut large ripe cucumbers into chunks. Put chunks into crock, and cover with brine of 1 gallon water to ½ cup salt. Leave overnight; then drain. Cover with fresh water and 1 tablespoon of alum per gallon. Heat cucumbers to boiling; then turn heat down as low as possible, and cook for about 2 hours. Drain, and chill in cold water. Drain.

Bring to boil a syrup of 2 pounds sugar to 1 pint vinegar, 6 tea-spoons whole cloves, and 2 sticks of cinnamon. Add pickles, and simmer until pickles appear transparent. Remove from stove, cover, and leave overnight. Reheat, and cook for 15 minutes for 3 more mornings. On the fourth morning, pack into jars, and process 5 minutes for pints in boiling water bath.

Salt Pickles (Dills)

Fill a clean crock to within 4 or 5 inches from the top with clean, small, whole cucumbers. Cover top with a ½ inch layer of salt; then cover cucumbers with fresh, cold water. Cover and weight down as previously mentioned, and leave in a cool place for about 3 weeks. Drain pickles, and rinse. Put the pickles back in the crock, layering them with the fol-lowing spices: Dill weed, whole mixed pickling spices, oregano, thyme, basil, and whole peppercorns. Bring to boil enough brine to cover the pickles using the following proportions: 1 cup water to 1 cup vinegar to ¼ cup salt. Cover, weight, and leave for at least 1 month. Pack and process as above.

Sandwich Slices

In a crock, place 1 gallon of sliced cucumbers. Pour 1½ cups salt over slices, and cover with cold water. Cover, weight, and leave overnight. Drain. Bring to a boil 4½ pints vinegar and 4½ pints water. Add cucumber slices, and simmer 5 to 10 minutes. Do not cook until tender. Drain well, discarding this liquid. Bring to a boil 1½ quarts vinegar,

3 cups water, 3 cups white sugar, 3 cups brown sugar, and 1½ teaspoons each mustard seed, celery seed, and turmeric. Pour over pickle slices, and leave 3 days. Pack as usual, and process for 10 minutes in boiling water bath.

Sweet Pickles

Pack clean, whole cucumbers to within 4–5 inches from the top of a clean crock. Make enough of the following brine to cover cucumbers: 1 gallon of boiling water to 1 pint salt. Pour hot brine over pickles, and leave 1 week. Drain pickles; cover again with boiling water with 1 table-spoon powdered alum added.

Repeat for two more mornings using fresh water and alum each time. Drain, cut each pickle in half lengthwise, and pack in jars. Bring to a boil 2 pints sugar and 2½ pints vinegar, and pour over pickles (be sure jars are hot). Next morning, drain, reheat, and add same amount of sugar as you have liquid. Add 1 teaspoon mixed pickling spices and ½ teaspoon celery seed to each quart of pickles. Pour boiling liquid over pickles, adjust lids, and process for 20 minutes in boiling water bath.

Sweet Cooked Pickles

Pack 7 pounds clean, medium-sized cucumbers in a crock, and cover with the following brine: 2 cups salt to 1 gallon water. Cover, weight as usual, and let set for 3 days. Drain, and cover pickles with clear water. Repeat clear water bath for 2 more days. Cut pickles into chunks, and cook about 2 hours in 1 part vinegar to 2 parts water; then drain.

Heat 3 pints vinegar and 3 pounds brown or white sugar or half of each, and pour over pickles, adding 2 teaspoons celery seed, 2 teaspoons whole cloves, 1 stick cinnamon, and ½ teaspoon powered alum. Reheat for 2 more mornings. Don't boil, just simmer. Drain, pack chunks into jars, cover with hot brine, and process 20 minutes for quarts, 10 for pints.

Sweet Easy Crock Pickles

In a clean crock, mix the following: 1 gallon vinegar, ¼ cup dry mustard, ½ cup salt, 1 tablespoon ground ginger, ½ cup whole cloves, 6 sticks of cinnamon (broken up), ½ cup peppercorns, and 1½ pounds brown sugar. Add 2 large onions (sliced) and 6 quarts of whole, small cucumbers. Add more vinegar if cucumbers aren't covered. Cover as usual, and leave for 1 to 3 months. Don't eat before one month. At the end of that time, they can be packed as usual and processed 5 minutes for pints and 15 for quarts.

Sweet Gherkins

First day: Pack 5 quarts of small, whole cucumbers into a 2-gallon crock. Cover with boiling water. That afternoon, drain, and cover with fresh boiling water.

Second day: Drain, and cover with fresh boiling water. That afternoon, drain, add ½ cup salt, and cover with fresh boiling water.

Third day: Drain, and prick cucumbers with table fork. Then make syrup using 3 cups vinegar and 3 cups sugar, and add 2 teaspoons whole mixed pickling spices, 2 teaspoons celery seed, ¾ teaspoon turmeric, and 8 small pieces of stick cinnamon. Heat to boiling, and pour over pickles. Pickles will not be covered with liquid at this stage. That afternoon, drain, adding 2 more cups vinegar and 2 more cups sugar. Heat to boiling, and pour over pickles.

Fourth day: Drain syrup into pan adding 2 cups sugar and 1 cup vinegar. Heat to boiling and pour over pickles. That afternoon, drain off syrup, adding 1 more cup sugar, and heat to boiling. Pack pickles into jars, cover with boiling syrup, adjust lids, and process in boiling water bath for 5 minutes for pints.

Sweet Icicle Pickles

Cut cucumbers into chunks or lengthwise quarters, and place in large crock. Cover cucumbers with a boiling brine of 2 cups salt to each gallon of water. Cover, weight, and leave one week. Drain, cover with fresh boiling water, and let stand 24 hours. Drain, add 1 tablespoon alum to each gallon of boiling water, and cover again. Let stand 24 hours; drain.

Make a syrup of 5 pounds sugar, 2½ quarts of vinegar, and 2 tablespoons whole allspice for each gallon of water it took to cover the cucumbers. (No water is added to this syrup; simply use these proportions to cover the amount of pickles.) Heat to boiling, and pour over pickles. Cover, and let stand 24 hours. Drain, bring syrup to boiling, and pour over pickles. Repeat this last step for 4 more days. Pack pickles into jars, strain syrup, and heat to boiling. Pour hot syrup over pickles in jars, adjust lids, and process in boiling water bath for 10 minutes for both pints and quarts.

Sweet Red Pickles

Peel, seed, and cube large, ripe cucumbers until you have about 2 gallons. Place these in a crock, sprinkle ½ cup salt over them, and cover with water. Leave overnight; then drain. Make syrup of 1 pint vinegar to 3¼ cups sugar, 1 teaspoon whole cloves, and 2 sticks of cinnamon (broken up). Heat to boiling, pour over cucumbers, and let stand overnight. Simmer cucumbers in syrup until tender. At the last minute, add 1 small (4-ounce) jar of maraschino cherries and juice. (More red food coloring can be added if needed.) Pack into hot jars, and process for 5 minutes for pints in boiling water bath.

Virginia Sweet Pickles

Put 3 gallons of clean, 4–5-inch cucumbers in a large crock. Cover with a brine of 2 cups salt to each gallon of water, and leave 1 week. Drain off brine, and cover cucumbers with boiling water. Leave for 24 hours, and then drain again. Split the pickles, and cover again with boiling water, adding 1½ heaping teaspoons of powdered alum. Leave another 24 hours; then drain again. Boil 3 quarts vinegar and 6 cups sugar until sugar is dissolved, and pour over pickles. Leave another 24 hours. Pour off vinegar, and add 3 cups sugar. Boil until sugar is dissolved, and pour over pickles. Let stand 24 hours. Drain and add 2 cups sugar, boiling until sugar is dissolved. Pack pickles in clean, hot jars adding 1 teaspoon mixed pickling spices to each jar, and cover with hot vinegar. Adjust lids, and process 20 minutes in boiling water bath.

SHORT-CUT PICKLES

These pickles take much less time to make than the previous brined pickles. Most of these recipes can be completed overnight, but some take 2 days. Most are also brined in that they are soaked in a salt-water brine overnight. Some of the recipes are then canned the next morning; others have almost as many steps as the brined pickles. The times, however, have been shortened to an hour or two between steps. There won't be a scum problem with any of these recipes, but you will have to cover and weight some of them as with the brined pickles.

Bread and Butter Pickles

Thinly slice 4 quarts of cucumbers and about 8 large white onions. Sprinkle with ½ cup salt, cover with ice cubes, and let stand 3 hours.

Drain. Bring to a boil 5 cups sugar, 5 cups vinegar, 1½ teaspoons turmeric, 2 teaspoons celery seed, and 3 tablespoons mustard seed. Add cucumber and onion slices, and cook 5 minutes. Pack into pint jars, and process for 5 minutes in boiling water bath.

> NOTE: Any one or all of the following items can also be added to basic bread and butter pickles: 2 sliced, sweet green or red peppers, ½ teaspoon cloves, 1 teaspoon ginger, and ½ teaspoon white pepper.

Chunky Pickles

Cut cucumbers into 1 inch chunks, and cover with a brine of 1 cup salt to 1 gallon of water. Cover, and let stand 5 or 6 hours. Bring to boil 2 cups vinegar, 2½ cups sugar, 4 tablespoons mustard seed, and 1 tablespoon celery seed. Add cucumber chunks, and cook 3 minutes. Pack into hot pint jars, and process for 10 minutes in boiling water bath.

Cucumber and Onion Pickles

Thinly slice 12 large cucumbers and 12 large onions. Sprinkle with 1 cup salt, and leave overnight. Drain, and rinse with cold water; then drain again. Make a syrup of 2 pounds brown sugar, 2 quarts vinegar, 1 teaspoon turmeric, 1 teaspoon mustard seed, and 2 teaspoons celery seed. Add cucumber and onion slices, and cook about 25 minutes. Pack into hot jars, cover with boiling liquid, and process for 5 minutes for pint jars in a boiling water bath.

Cucumber Slices

Slice small (not over 5 inches) cucumbers in thin ⅛ inch slices. Mix with ½ cup salt, and leave 4 hours. Drain. Bring to a boil 3 cups vinegar, 4 cups water, and 3 teaspoons turmeric. Pour over cucumbers, and let stand until liquid is cold. Drain. Rinse cucumbers in cold water, and drain.

Bring to boil 1 cup water, 4 cups vinegar, 2 cups sugar, 1 tablespoon mustard seed, 1 teaspoon whole cloves, 1 piece ginger root, and 2 sticks cinnamon (broken up). Pour over cucumbers, and leave 24 hours. Drain cucumbers, straining liquid into kettle. Add 2 cups brown sugar, and bring to a boil. Add cucumbers, and cook about 10 minutes; then pack into pint jars, and process for 10 minutes in boiling water bath.

Curry Pickles

Thinly slice 6 large peeled cucumbers, 6 large onions, 3 large sweet red peppers, and 3 large sweet green peppers. Sprinkle with ½ cup salt, and cover with cold water. Let stand overnight; then drain. Bring to a boil 1 pint vinegar, ½ pint water, 2 pounds sugar, 3 tablespoons mixed pickling spices, and 2 tablespoons celery salt. Add vegetable slices, and cook 10 minutes. Stir in 1 teaspoon curry powder, fill pint jars, and process for 5 minutes in boiling water bath.

Kosher-Style Dills

Cover medium-sized cucumbers with a brine of ½ cup salt to each quart of water. Leave 24 hours; then drain. Make a canning solution of 2 cups white vinegar to 3 cups water. Add 2 tablespoons mixed pickling spices, and bring to a boil. Add cucumbers, and remove from heat. Pack cucumbers into hot quart jars along with a couple cloves of garlic, a couple hot peppers, and a few sprigs of dill. Return vinegar to stove, and heat to boiling. Pour over cucumbers, adjust lids, and process for 20 minutes in boiling water bath.

Olive Oil Pickles

Thinly slice 3 quarts of cucumbers. Put in layers in glass bowl with ½ cup salt, and leave overnight. Drain, and rinse well with clear, fresh water. Bring to a boil 1 quart vinegar, ½ cup olive oil, ½ cup sugar, 4 tablespoons mustard seed, and 4 tablespoons celery seed. Add cucumber slices, and cook slowly until slices change color. Pack into hot jars, and process pint jars for 5 minutes in boiling water bath.

Sweet Lime Pickles

Slice about 12 to 15 medium-sized cucumbers into thin slices. Dissolve 2 cups lime (calcium hydroxide) in 2 gallons of water, and pour over cucumber slices. Let stand 24 hours; then drain. Cover slices with clear water, let stand 3 hours, then drain.

Dissolve 4 pounds of sugar in ½ gallon of vinegar, and add 2 teaspoons whole cloves and 1 teaspoon salt. Pour over cucumbers, and leave overnight. Pack in jars, cover with boiling syrup, and process for 5 minutes for pints in a boiling water bath.

Whole Dills

Cover 3- to 5-inch whole cucumbers with a brine of ¾ cup salt to 1 gallon water, and leave overnight. Drain. Pack cucumbers into quart jars, and add dill and 2 teaspoons mustard seed to each jar. Heat to boiling 3 pints vinegar, 4½ pints water, ¼ cup sugar, ¾ cup salt, and 2 tablespoons mixed pickling spices. Pour over pickles and process quart jars for 20 minutes.

> *NOTE:* Pickling spices can be tied in a cloth bag and cooked with the vinegar solution, then removed to make liquid in pickle jars clearer.

Whole Sweet-Sour Pickles

Place about 4 pounds of small 3- to 4-inch cucumbers in a large container. Dissolve 1 cup sugar in ½ gallon of boiling water. Pour over cucumbers, and leave until liquid cools; then drain. Bring to a boil 3 pints vinegar, 1 pint water, 3 cups sugar, and 1 tablespoon mixed pickling spices. Pour over cucumbers, and leave 24 hours. Bring to a boil, pack hot into pint jars, and process for 5 minutes in boiling water bath.

Yellow Chunk Pickles

Peel ripe, yellow cucumbers, cut in half to remove seeds, and then cut into chunks. Soak overnight in water. Bring the following ingredients to a boil: 1 quart white vinegar, 1 pint water, 2 cups sugar, 1 teaspoon mustard seed, and 2 teaspoons mixed pickling spices. Add cucumbers, and boil for 5 minutes. Pack cucumbers into hot pint jars adding 1 teaspoon of salt and a couple slices of onion to each jar. Cover with boiling liquid, and process for 5 minutes in boiling water bath.

> *NOTE:* This recipe can also be used with sliced green cucumbers. Cider vinegar can take the place of white vinegar if using the darker-colored cucumbers.

IN-THE-JAR PICKLES

These, of course, are the simplest pickles to make. Most recipes are simply fresh cucumbers packed into jars covered with a hot, spiced vinegar solution. With these recipes, any number of jars of pickles may be canned—from a single half-pint to 20 quarts. Just make whatever amount of the vinegar solution you will need to cover the pickles. Try several of the recipes, and familiarize yourself and your family with homemade pickles and the taste of the various spices. When you know what your family likes best, you can then make some of the longer versions containing similar ingredients.

Dill Pickles (1)

Cut cucumbers in half lengthwise, and pack into jars. Add 2 tablespoons dill seed and 3 peppercorns to each jar. Heat to boiling a canning solution of 1 cup vinegar to 1 cup water to 2 tablespoons salt. Pour over cucumbers, and process pint jars for 15 minutes in boiling water bath.

Dill Pickles (2)

Clean medium-sized cucumbers, and slice; cut into spears or chunks. Cover prepared cucumbers with ice, and leave a few hours, adding more ice as needed. Pack into clean pint jars, and add the following to each jar: pinch of alum, sprig of dill, ½ teaspoon dill seed, pinch turmeric, cayenne peppers (¼ to ½ of a dried or fresh pepper), 1 or 2 cloves of garlic, and ½ teaspoon mustard seed.

Using the following proportions, bring enough liquid to a boil to cover the pickles: 1 quart vinegar, 2 quarts water, and 1 cup salt. Pour boiling liquid over cucumbers, adjust lids, and process 5 minutes for pints. Warm jars for the boiling liquid by setting in a pan of hot water.

Dill Slices

Slice cucumbers, and pack into jars. Cover cucumbers with cold water, and leave overnight. Drain. Heat to boiling 6 quarts water, 2 cups salt, 1 teaspoon alum, and 1 quart vinegar. To top of each jar of cucumbers, add 2 cloves garlic, 6 green grapes, and a pinch of turmeric, dill head, or weed, or one heaping teaspoon of dill seed. Cover with boiling liquid, and process pint jars for 5 minutes in boiling water bath.

Ice Water Chunks

Cut medium-sized cucumbers into chunks, cover with ice water for 2 to 3 hours, and drain. Pack into jars, adding 3 tiny whole onions, 1 piece of celery, and 1 teaspoon mustard seed to each jar. Cover with a boiling solution of 1 cup sugar to 1 quart vinegar to ⅓ cup salt. Process pint jars for 5 minutes in boiling water bath.

Kosher-Style Dills

Place a layer of dill, 1 clove of garlic, and 1½ teaspoons mustard seed in the bottom of each jar. Fill with whole, small cucumbers. Add another layer of dill on top of each jar. Cover with a boiling solution of 1 cup water to 1 cup vinegar to 2 tablespoons salt. Process pint jars for 20 minutes in boiling water bath. Pickles will shrivel at first but will plump up later.

Sweet Cucumber Slices

Simmer 4 quarts cucumber slices in 1 quart vinegar, 3 tablespoons salt, 3 teaspoons mustard seed, and ¼ cup sugar for 15 minutes. Drain, discard liquid, and pack slices into hot jars. Heat to boiling 3½ cups vinegar, 5½ cups sugar, 3 teaspoons celery seed, and 3 teaspoons whole allspice. Pour over pickles, and process pint jars for 5 minutes in boiling water bath.

Sweet Dills

Slice 5 quarts of cucumbers. Place one dill head in each jar, and pack with cucumber slices. Heat to boiling 3 pints vinegar, 6 cups sugar, ¾ cup salt, 2 teaspoons celery seed, and 2 teaspoons mustard seed. Pour over cucumbers, and put another dill head on top of each jar. Process pint jars for 5 minutes in boiling water bath.

Sweet Sticks

Cut firm, medium-sized cucumbers into quarters lengthwise. Cover with boiling water, and leave a few hours. Drain, and pack into jars. Boil for 5 minutes a solution of 1 quart vinegar, 5 cups sugar, 3 tablespoons salt, and 1 tablespoon each of celery seed, mustard seed, and turmeric. Cover pickles, and process pint jars for 5 minutes in boiling water bath.

VEGETABLE PICKLES

Bean Pickles

Pack stemmed, whole green beans into jars. Add ¼ teaspoon cayenne pepper (or small hot pepper), 1 clove garlic, and 1 head of fresh dill or

½ teaspoon dill seed. Bring to boil 1¼ cups vinegar, 1¼ cups water, and 2 tablespoons salt. Pour over beans, and process pint jars for 10 minutes.

Pickled Beets

Wash small, young beets, leaving on root end and at least 2 inches of top. Cook until tender; then remove skins and ends. Leave small beets whole, but larger ones can be quartered, sliced, or cubed. Bring to a boil a syrup of 2 cups sugar, 2 cups water, 2 cups vinegar, 1 teaspoon cloves, 1 teaspoon allspice, and 1 tablespoon cinnamon. Add beets, and boil 10 minutes. Pack into hot jars, and process quart jars for 30 minutes.

Dilled Brussels Sprouts

Cook Brussels sprouts until tender–crisp in salted water, and pack into jars. Add 1 slice onion, small hot pepper, garlic clove, and dill head to each jar. Bring to boil 1 cup vinegar, 1 cup water, and 2 tablespoons salt. Pour over Brussels sprouts, and process pints for 10 minutes. Use these whole as appetizer or relish, or use sliced in salads.

Carrot Pickles

Peel carrots; then slice, or cut into sticks. Cook in small amount of salted water for about 5 minutes; then drain. Bring to a boil 2 cups vinegar, 1½ cups water, 1½ cups sugar, about 20 whole cloves, 4 sticks of cinnamon (broken up), and 1 tablespoon salt. Pack carrots into hot jars, and cover with liquid. Leave ½ inch headspace, and process pints and quarts for 30 minutes.

Pickled Cauliflower

Break cauliflower into flowerettes, and simmer in a small amount of salted water until tender–crisp. Drain, and pack into jars, adding a small hot pepper, a garlic clove, and head of dill to each jar. Cover with a boiling solution of 1 cup white vinegar to 1 cup water to 2 tablespoons salt. Process pint jars for 10 minutes.

Mixed Vegetable Pickles

Use equal parts of any or all of these vegetables:

    sliced cucumbers
    sliced sweet peppers
    chopped cabbage or whole Brussels sprouts

    sliced onions or whole, small pickling onions
    quartered green tomatoes
    sliced carrots
    green or yellow beans, 1-inch pieces
    chopped celery
    cauliflower, broken into flowerettes

Cover vegetables with a brine of 1 cup salt to 1 gallon water, and leave them overnight. Drain. Bring to a boil a canning solution of 1 hot pepper (later removed), 2 tablespoons mustard seed, 1 tablespoon celery seed, 2 cups sugar, and 6½ cups vinegar. Add vegetables, and simmer 5 minutes. Pack into jars, and process pint jars for 15 minutes in boiling water bath.

Okra Pickles

Pack firm, small okra pods into jars. Place a garlic bud, ½ teaspoon dill seed, and a small hot pepper, if desired, on top of each jar. Bring to boil a brine of 1 cup white vinegar, 2 cups water, and 3 tablespoons salt. Pour over okra, and process pint jars for 10 minutes.

Pickled Onions

To peel the tiny pickling onions, cover them with boiling water, and leave them for 2 minutes. Drain, dip in cold water, then peel. Sprinkle onions with salt (4 tablespoons salt per quart of onions), cover with water, and leave them overnight. Drain and rinse.

    Pack onions into pint jars with a small hot pepper and 1 bay leaf in each jar. Bring to a boil 1 cup sugar, 1 quart white vinegar, 1 tablespoon prepared horseradish, and 2 tablespoons mustard seed. Pour over onions, and process pint jars for 10 minutes in boiling water bath.

Jalapeno Peppers

Pack whole peppers (leaving stems on) into jars. Bring to boiling 2 cups vinegar, ½ cup water, ½ cup olive oil, 1 teaspoon salt, and 2 teaspoons whole mixed pickling spices (optional). Pour over peppers leaving 1 inch of headspace. Process for 10 minutes.

Pickled Peppers

Wear rubber gloves when handling hot peppers. They can burn your hands while you're picking them, as well as when chopping. Use any long red, yellow, or green peppers, and cut two small slits in each pepper. Cover peppers with a brine of 2 quarts water to ¾ cup salt, and let stand overnight. Drain and rinse. Bring to a boil 1 cup water, 5 cups vinegar, 2 tablespoons sugar, 1 tablespoon horseradish, and 1 garlic clove. Add peppers and simmer 15 minutes. Pack peppers into hot jars, cover with boiling liquid (remove garlic clove), and process pint jars for 10 minutes.

Canned Pimentos

Boil pimentos 3 to 5 minutes or until skins slip easily. Remove skin, stem, blossom end, and seeds with a sharp knife. Flatten and pack pimentos horizontally in half-pint jars. Leave ½ inch headspace, and add no liquid. Process for 35 minutes in boiling water bath.

Green Tomato Dills

Quarter green tomatoes, and pack into quart jars. Add 2 cloves of garlic and head of dill to each jar. Bring to boil a canning solution of 1 quart vinegar to 2 quarts water to 1 cup salt. Let boil 5 minutes; then pour over tomatoes, and process quart jars for 15 minutes in boiling water bath.

Sweet Green Tomato Pickles

Sprinkle 4 tablespoons salt over 1 gallon sliced green tomatoes, and leave them overnight. Drain; then cover tomatoes with 1½ teaspoons alum and 2 quarts boiling water. Leave them about 30 minutes. Drain, and rinse in cold water.

Bring to a boil 1½ cups vinegar, ½ cup water, 2 cups sugar, 1½ teaspoons mixed pickling spices, 1½ teaspoons celery seed, 1½ teaspoons mustard seed, and ¼ teaspoon each of ground allspice and cinnamon. Pour over tomato slices, and leave them overnight. Drain, reheat to boiling, and pour over tomatoes. Drain; reheat to boiling. Pack slices into hot jars, cover with boiling liquid, and process pint jars for 5 minutes.

Zucchini Slices

Thinly slice 1 gallon unpeeled zucchini and 1 quart onions. Bring to a boil 2 quarts vinegar, 4 cups sugar, 1 cup salt, 1 tablespoon celery seed, 1 tablespoon turmeric, and 2 teaspoons dry mustard. *For Dilled Zucchini,* add 1 tablespoon dill seeds. Pour over zucchini, and leave 1 hour. Bring to a boil, and cook 3 minutes. Pack into hot jars, and process pint jars for 5 minutes in boiling water bath.

RELISHES

Chow-Chow

> 2 quarts chopped cabbage
> 6 cups coarsely chopped green and red peppers
> 4 cups chopped onions
> 4 cups chopped green tomatoes
> 3 chopped hot peppers (optional)

Mix vegetables with 4 tablespoons salt, cover, and leave overnight. Drain. Combine 6 cups vinegar, 2 cups sugar, 1 tablespoon dry mustard, and 1 teaspoon ginger. Simmer for 10 minutes; then add vegetables, and simmer for about 15 minutes. Pack hot in hot jars, and process pint jars for 5 minutes.

Corn Relish

Boil approximately $1\frac{1}{2}$ dozen ears of fresh sweet corn for 5 minutes; then plunge into ice water to cool. Cut from cob, and measure about 10 cups. Add 2 sweet green peppers and 2 sweet red peppers coarsely chopped, 1 cup chopped onions, 1 cup chopped celery, $1\frac{1}{2}$ cups sugar, 2 table-

Left, chopped onions, green pepper and celery are needed in addition to corn for corn relish. *Right,* the ingredients are mixed together with spices, sugar and vinegar and simmered 20 minutes.

spoons mustard seed, 1 tablespoon salt, 1 teaspoon turmeric, 1 teaspoon celery seed, 2 cups water, and 3 cups white vinegar. Simmer for 15 to 20 minutes, pack hot into pint jars, and process for 15 minutes.

Ripe Cucumber Relish

Peel large, ripe yellow cucumbers, cut in half lengthwise, and remove seeds. Dice cucumbers; then dice an equal amount of onions. Stir in salt (2 teaspoons per pint). Cover, and let stand overnight. Drain. Add diced celery and sweet peppers. Cover vegetables with a canning solution of 1 pint vinegar to 2 cups sugar to 1 tablespoon mustard seeds. Simmer vegetables until mixture thickens and cucumbers are golden. Pack into hot pint jars, and process for 5 minutes.

End-of-Garden Relish

Combine the following vegetables with ½ cup salt, and leave them overnight: 8 cups chopped green tomatoes, 4 cups peeled chopped red tomatoes, 4 cups chopped cabbage, 3 cups chopped onions, 2 cups chopped celery, 1 cup each of sweet red and green peppers chopped, and 1 cup chopped cucumbers. Drain. Simmer the following for 10 minutes: 8 cups vinegar, 4 cups brown sugar, and 1 tablespoon mustard seed. Add vegetables, and simmer for 30 minutes. Pack hot into jars, and process pints for 15 minutes.

Mixed Vegetable Relish

Cook the following vegetables until tender in a small amount of salted water: 2 cups each of sliced carrots, lima beans, cauliflower (broken into flowerettes), corn, small pickling onions (or 1 cup diced onion), green beans cut in 1-inch pieces, 5 cups small cucumbers cut in 1-inch slices, 1 cup chopped celery, and 3 cups sweet green or red peppers coarsely chopped. Drain vegetables, add vinegar to cover them and 2 cups sugar, ½ teaspoon salt, and 4 tablespoons mustard seed. Boil for 10 minutes; then pack into hot jars, and process pint jars for 15 minutes.

Hot Pepper Relish

Wear rubber gloves when working with hot peppers. Remove seeds from red and green chili peppers; then coarsely chop. Add an equal amount of chopped onions. Mix well, and stir in ½ teaspoon salt per pint of vegetables. Cover with boiling water, and let stand for 15 minutes. Drain, and discard liquid. Cover vegetables with a canning solution of equal parts vinegar and sugar; then simmer for 20 minutes. Pack into hot jars, and process pint jars for 5 minutes.

Red Pepper Relish

Grind or finely chop sweet red peppers. Stir in salt (2 teaspoons per pint), and let stand 3 hours. Add sugar and vinegar, and simmer until thick (2 cups sugar and 1⅓ cup vinegar per pint). Pour hot into hot jars, and process pint jars for 10 minutes in boiling water bath.

Sweet Pepper Slaw

Coarsely chop 2 large cabbage heads and 1 dozen each of sweet green peppers, sweet red peppers, and onions. Stir in 4 tablespoons salt, and leave them overnight. Drain. Stir in 2 tablespoons celery seed, 2 tablespoons mustard seed, and 6 cups sugar. Cover with vinegar. Bring to a boil, and cook for 20 minutes. Pack into hot jars, and process pint jars for 5 minutes in boiling water bath.

Piccalilli

Stir 4 tablespoons salt into 1 quart chopped cabbage, 1 quart chopped green tomatoes, 1 cup each of sweet green and red peppers chopped, and 2 large onions chopped. Leave them overnight; then drain in a bag squeezing slightly. Boil for 5 minutes 2 cups vinegar, 2 cups water, 2 cups brown sugar, 1 tablespoon celery seed, 2 teaspoons ground cinnamon, ½ teaspoon ground cloves, and 1 teaspoon dry mustard. Add vegetables, and simmer for 3 minutes. Pack into hot jars, and process for 10 minutes.

Tomato Relish

Coarsely chop the following vegetables and put in a heavy pan: 1 gallon peeled red tomatoes, 3 large onions, 2 sweet peppers (seeded), and 1 cup celery. Add 1 pint vinegar, 1½ cups brown sugar, 2 tablespoons salt, 3 tablespoons mustard seed, and 2 tablespoons ground cinnamon. Cook slowly until mixture becomes thick and clear. Pour into hot jars, and process pint jars for 5 minutes in boiling water bath.

Zucchini Relish

Combine the following ingredients in a heavy pan: 5 quarts coarsely ground zucchini, about 6 large onions ground, 2 large sweet peppers ground, 1 tablespoon salt, 1 teaspoon turmeric, 1 tablespoon celery seed, 1 teaspoon pepper, 4 cups vinegar, and 1 cup sugar. Simmer for 15 minutes. Process pint jars for 10 minutes in boiling water bath.

FRUIT PICKLES AND RELISHES

Pickled Apricots

Use firm, slightly underripe apricots. Do not remove skins. Stick 3 or 4 cloves into each apricot. Bring to boil 4 cups white sugar, 4 cups brown sugar, 4 cups vinegar, and 6 sticks of cinnamon. Add apricots, and cook gently one layer at a time until tender. Pack apricots into jars, adding 1 stick of cinnamon to each jar; then cover with boiling syrup. Process pint jars for 20 minutes.

Cantaloupe Pickles

Peel underripe cantaloupes, and cut into 1 inch cubes. Make a spice bag containing 1 teaspoon whole allspice, 2 sticks cinnamon, and 2 teaspoons whole cloves. Combine 4 cups vinegar, 2 cups water, and spice bag. Bring to boiling, and pour over cantaloupe. Let stand overnight; then drain. Bring liquid to a boil; then add 4 cups sugar and cantaloupe pieces. Cook until pieces are transparent. Pack into hot jars, and process pint jars for 5 minutes.

Crabapple Pickles

Use firm crabapples that are uniform in size. Prick the skin in several places, or run a long needle through the apples to keep them from bursting. Leave stems intact. Make a cheesecloth bag containing 1 tablespoon whole cloves, 3 sticks of cinnamon (broken up), and 1 tablespoon whole allspice. Combine 3 cups vinegar, 3 cups water, and 6 cups sugar. Add spice bag, and boil for 5 minutes. Add crabapples, and cook gently until almost tender. Cook only one layer at a time, and handle them gently.

When all the apples are cooked, pour the syrup and spices over the apples, and let stand overnight. Pack crabapples into hot jars, and cover with boiling syrup. Process pint jars for 20 minutes in boiling water bath.

Pickled Peaches

Pare peaches, and drop into a solution of 1 tablespoon salt to 1 tablespoon vinegar to 2 quarts water. Make a spice bag containing 3 sticks cinnamon, 1 tablespoon whole cloves, 1 tablespoon whole allspice, and a piece of ginger root. Bring to a boil 2 cups sugar, 2 cups water, and 3 cups vinegar. Add spice bag and peaches, and cook for 5 minutes. Remove from stove, cover, and leave for 4 hours. Add 2 cups sugar, heat to boiling, then cover, and let stand overnight. Pack peaches in jars. Add 1 cup sugar to syrup, heat to boiling, and pour over pickles. Process pints and quarts for 20 minutes in boiling water bath.

Pickled Pears

Peel pears, but leave them whole and with stem intact. After peeling pears, drop them in a solution of 1 tablespoon vinegar to 1 quart water. Make a spice bag containing 1 tablespoon mixed pickling spices, 1 teaspoon whole cloves, 3 sticks of cinnamon, and 1 teaspoon whole ginger root. Bring to a boil 3 cups sugar, 3 cups water, 2 cups vinegar, and ½ lemon thinly sliced. Add pears, and cook gently one layer at a time until tender. Pour boiling syrup over pears, and let stand overnight. Pack pears into jars, cover with boiling syrup, and process pints and quarts for 15 minutes.

Rhubarb Sauce

Combine 8 cups chopped rhubarb, ½ cup chopped onion, 2 cups chopped raisins, 4 cups brown sugar, and ½ cup vinegar, and cook until thick. Add 1 teaspoon each of ground cinnamon, ground ginger, and ground allspice, and cook for 5 more minutes. Pack into jars, and process for 15 minutes.

Watermelon Pickles

Remove rind and all pink from one watermelon rind. Cut into 1-inch squares. Soak rind overnight in a brine of 1 cup salt to 1 gallon water. Drain, and rinse in cold water. Cover with cold water, and cook until fork–tender; then drain.

Left, to prepare watermelon pickles, first start with a thick-skinned melon. Remove all the pink and green from the rind and dice the white portion into 1 inch chunks. *Right,* after cooking, pack into clean, hot jars adding one stick of cinnamon to each jar. Process in boiling water bath canner.

Make a spice bag containing 1 tablespoon whole cloves and 6 sticks of cinnamon. Combine 8 cups sugar, 4 cups vinegar, 2 cups water, spice bag, and 1 lemon thinly sliced. Boil for 5 minutes, add watermelon rind, and cook until rind is translucent. Pack hot into jars, adding 1 stick of cinnamon to each jar, and process pint jars for 5 minutes.

SAUERKRAUT AND OTHER BRINED VEGETABLES

Although many vegetables have been preserved by curing in a brine solution, sauerkraut is probably the most well known. Sauerkraut was one of those early-time "health foods," as it was supposed to be a cure or preventive for scurvy. Naturally, because of its long-keeping qualities, it was popular with travelers such as sailors and settlers.

There are two basic methods of making kraut: The old-time "kraut barrel," and the newer method of making kraut in fruit jars. There are literally hundreds of different variations and recipes of these two methods.

Regardless of which method you choose, there are several rules to follow, not only for making kraut, but for any brined vegetable.

1. Make sure you follow directions carefully.
2. Use the exact amount of vegetable and ingredients as called for, weighing the amounts to be sure.
3. Use only good, sound, fresh produce.
4. Make sure the vegetables are covered with brine and are protected from insects and scum.
5. Use either pure or canning salt; don't use ordinary salt, which has iodine and starch added to it.
6. If any kraut or other brined vegetable becomes off-color, is soft, or has a bad odor, discard it. It isn't fit to eat.

If your garden has produced an overabundance of cabbage, or if you can get a good buy on cabbage at your local vegetable market, you'll probably want to make up some sauerkraut for the winter months.

Barrel Kraut

If you decide to make kraut in the old-fashioned way using a barrel or crock, you'll need either a 5-gallon stone crock or barrel. If you use a wooden barrel, don't use one made of pine as it will add an off-flavor to the kraut. The best barrels are old pickling barrels or used whiskey barrels. Before using a wooden barrel, it should be soaked in water for about a week to allow it to swell and tighten up. Some people like to paraffin wooden containers by warming the barrel and applying melted paraffin to it with a brush.

After picking and cleaning the cabbage (it takes about 45 pounds of cabbage to fill a 5-gallon crock), cut off all the outer wilted leaves. If the cabbage has been sprayed with insecticide, make sure you wash it thoroughly under cold, running water. Cut the cabbage head in half. We like to let them soak about a half hour in saltwater to kill any cabbage worms, which will float to the top of the water. Rinse in cold water again. Cut into quarters, and remove the core. The cabbage can be shredded into thin shreds using a sharp knife; however, it's much easier and faster to use a regular "kraut cutter." This is a long board with 2 knife blades placed on it at an angle. The board has small side strips that guide the cabbage heads across the cutters. These cutters are available at any store that sells canning supplies, and they will more than pay for themselves. Although they are much safer than using a kitchen knife, make sure you keep your fingers clear of the angled knives, or you may lose a fingernail or even part of a finger. For best results, the cabbage shreds should be consistently cut to the same size—about the thickness of a dime.

Place the shredded cabbage in a larger clean container, and fluff it around with your hands to break up the pieces that are clinging together. Don't, however, bruise the shreds. When you've shredded a pretty good amount of cabbage, weigh out 5 pounds on a kitchen scale. Sprinkle 3 tablespoons of pure granulated salt over the cabbage. Don't use iodized table salt. Mix the salt in thoroughly with the cabbage; then let it set for several minutes to allow it to wilt a bit. Place the salted cabbage shreds in the crock or barrel. Use either your hands, a wooden tamper such as a clean 2 x 4, or a wooden spoon to press the cabbage down firmly in the crock. The idea is to compact the cabbage but not to bruise it. You want the cabbage compressed just enough to force the juice to come to the surface. Repeat the shredding, salting, and packing until the crock or barrel is filled to within about 4 inches from the top. Some people like to sprinkle caraway seeds in the layers of cabbage; however, do so sparingly, using not more than ½ teaspoon for each gallon of cabbage.

The old-fashioned method of covering the kraut crock is to use a clean white muslin cloth or several layers of cheesecloth to cover the cabbage. Make sure the cloth covers all of the cabbage. Then a "follower" made of a plate or a hardwood paraffined board that just fits the inside of the crock is placed down over the cabbage, making sure there are no air spaces. A weight is placed on top of the follower to force the follower down, allowing the brine to come just to the follower but not over it. Some people like to use a glass fruit jar filled with water for the weight. By using this as a weight, you can readily adjust the amount of weight and pressure to correctly compress the follower in place. However, a better and newer method utilizes a large, heavy-duty plastic bag filled with water, which is used as both the follower and the weight. Make absolutely sure the bag is clean and will hold water; then fill with water, and merely place down over the shredded cabbage. The bag will settle down against the sides of the crock and over the cabbage, sealing out all air. By adding or subtracting water, you can adjust the weight to the proper compression so the brine just covers the shredded cabbage.

To ferment properly, kraut should be kept at a temperature of 68°F to 72°F. It will normally take about 5 to 6 weeks for the kraut to be completed. We like to make kraut about the middle of October,

Weight cabbage with a plate and water-filled jar or fill a plastic bag with water and use that for a weight.

because it is easier to maintain the proper temperature at that time. While the kraut is forming, a white scum will form on top of the brine. Some people suggest that you remove this scum daily. One method of doing this if using the cloth, is to carefully lift off the cloth and the scum at the same time. Wash the cloth in hot water using no soap; then rinse in cold water. If the brine drops below the kraut during the curing process, pour in a bit of fresh water to which a pinch or two of salt has been added.

After the kraut has stopped fermenting and bubbling, it's done and ready for eating. The old-fashioned method of storing was to merely place the kraut barrel or crock in a cold place, such as a root cellar, and take the amount of kraut needed directly out of the barrel. But each time you remove the follower, a bit of kraut on the top will spoil and has to be skimmed off. Today most people make kraut in the crock, and then store it in glass fruit jars.

To store in this manner, heat the kraut to 185°F to 210°F, but do not allow it to boil. Then pack the hot sauerkraut into clean, hot canning jars. Make sure kraut is covered with juice, and leave ½ inch headspace. Process using a boiling water bath for 15 minutes if you use pints, 20 minutes if you use quart jars. The processing time should start as soon as you place the hot jars in the boiling water. After processing, remove the jars from the boiling water, complete the seals if necessary, and allow to cool out of a draft.

Remove jars from canner and place on wire rack to cool.

MAKING KRAUT IN JARS

This second method of making kraut is a bit more modern and doesn't involve as much time, nor does it require the large crock, or even a large amount of cabbage. You can make as few or as many jars as you wish. This method does require glass jars with rubber rings and zinc caps.

The cabbage is washed, quartered and shredded just as before. Weigh cabbage, then place in a large pan and sprinkle with salt. It takes 2 teaspoons of salt per pound of cabbage. Again, mix together, then allow to set for a few minutes. Pack the cabbage firmly down into pint jars using a wooden spoon or pestle. Check for air bubbles in the cabbage and use a small wooden spoon to press out any that you find. Slip on rubber rings and screw zinc lids on loosely. Place the jars in an old pan or washtub as they will bubble and spew, and store in an area of about 70°F. It should take about 10 days for the sauerkraut to cure. The lids will probably bulge somewhat during the curing and kraut will spew out between the lid and the rubber rings. Wipe off any kraut that bubbles out and tighten the lid a bit more.

When the bubbling stops, the fermenting is through. Remove the lids and add a brine made of two tablespoons of salt per one quart of water. Just cover the kraut in each jar. Seal the jars and store in a cool place. Some people like to can the finished kraut for longer keeping and this is done following the instructions for the longer cure kraut.

SAUERKRAUT SPOILAGE

If you had trouble making sauerkraut, there may be several reasons. If the kraut was soft, there may have been too high a temperature during the fermentation period, not enough salt, or unevenly distributed salt. There may have been air pockets caused by faulty packing. If the kraut is dark, it may mean the cabbage was not washed or trimmed properly, or there wasn't enough juice to cover the cabbage during fermentation. Again, uneven distribution of salt as well as air or high temperatures during processing can cause dark kraut. Sometimes dark kraut is caused by storing too long.

If the kraut is pink in color, it may be caused by too much salt, a particular type of yeast, using iodized salt, overcooking, using iron utensils, or by minerals in the water.

BRINING OTHER VEGETABLES

In addition to cabbage, there are many other vegetables that can be brined. Turnips, or "turnip kraut" is an excellent substitute for cabbage kraut. Other vegetables include peppers, snap beans, carrots, beets, and cauliflower. These vegetables will add a somewhat different taste and look to your wintertime salads or relish trays.

Turnip Kraut

This is a real taste treat that both your family and guests will love. Use only fresh, young, purple-topped turnips. Remove skins, weigh out 10 pounds of turnips, and place in large bowl. Shred into fine, even pieces. Sprinkle 1/4 cup salt over the shredded turnips, and mix thoroughly. Pack firmly into a crock in the manner of sauerkraut. Keep the kraut at room temperature during curing, and make sure it is covered with a brine solution. After about 15 to 20 days, it should be done; it can then be placed in sterilized jars and processed as for sauerkraut.

The vegetables mentioned earlier can be brined quite simply. For snap beans, remove ends, and break into small lengths. Blanch for about 5 minutes in boiling water. To each 5 pounds of vegetables, use a brine mix of 1/2 cup salt and 1/2 cup vinegar. After mixing thoroughly, pack into crock, and cure as sauerkraut.

Another method of brining can be used for even more vegetables, and the brine is less salty tasting. You can use turnip or mustard greens, and turnips and rutabagas as well for this cure. Prepare all vegetables as you would for table use, washing greens thoroughly, slicing and dicing turnips, etc. Break cauliflower into individual flowerettes. Blanch for 5 minutes in boiling water; then cool quickly. To make up the brine solution, add ½ pound salt and 1 cup of 5% acetic acid vinegar to each gallon of water. Place the vegetables in clean crocks until each crock is almost full; then cover with cheesecloth, follower, and weight as for sauerkraut. Pour brine mix over vegetables to just cover them. Place in a cool place, and cure as for sauerkraut. After they have completed the cure, you can remove, pack into jars, and process as for sauerkraut.

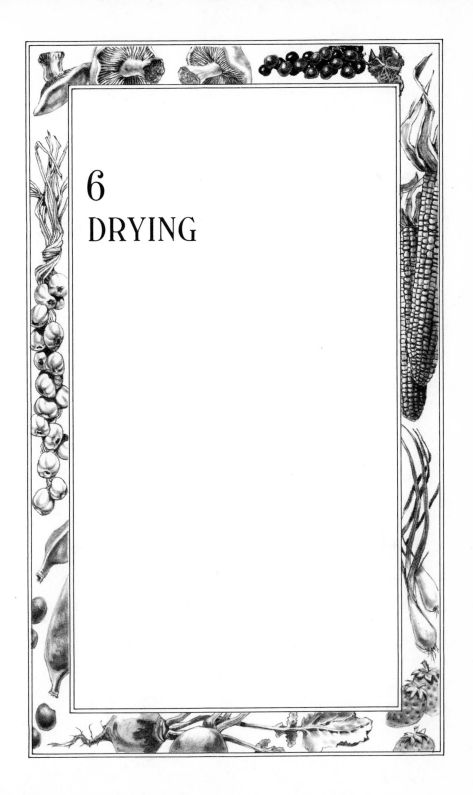

6
DRYING

Drying, or to be more "scientific" *dehydrating,* is probably the oldest form of food preservation known to man. It was a food preservation method universally practiced by the American Indian and is still used today by many primitive peoples to preserve food for storage. Some of the earlier dried foods included figs and dates, spices from the Orient, and even fish and meat. There are several advantages to drying, but probably the most important is the simplicity of preserving food in this method. The simplest method of drying, sun drying, requires only a few trays, something to cover them with, and several days of hot dry weather. Compare this with the equipment and time needed to prepare food for storage by canning.

Many people learned to dry food for storage during World War II when canning supplies and sugar were short, but with the popularity of the home freezer, drying sort of fell by the wayside. Today with the uncertainties we live with, drying is once again becoming more popular as a method of preserving food. Dried food takes up much less space than frozen or canned food. A bushel of fresh produce can often be dehydrated into a small container the size of a quart fruit jar. Another advantage of drying is that no electricity is required to keep the food, as in frozen foods, and little or no energy is required to process the foods, as in canning.

Another advantage is the convenience of dried foods; you don't have to thaw out the foods, and you won't have any leftovers. Merely take out what you need, reclose the container of dried food, and reconstitute the food you have removed.

Dried food can easily be taken on a camping or hiking trip. The small bags of lightweight food can be carried on backpacking or canoe camping trips. Dried munching food such as jerky, dried apples, and peaches have been popular with hunters for years, and a few nibbles of these foods can keep you going all day.

Drying has few disadvantages, but one is that dried food doesn't taste at all like its fresh counterpart. It has a completely different taste all its own. This is not necessarily bad—merely different. You and your family will have to experiment to decide which foods you like best dried. There are basically 3 ways of drying: sun drying, oven drying, and drying with specially constructed or purchased dehydrators.

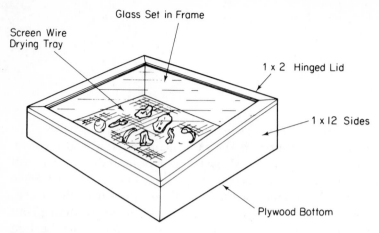

Glass Set in Frame

Screen Wire
Drying Tray

1 x 2 Hinged Lid

1 x 12 Sides

Plywood Bottom

Solar dryer.

For sun drying, you will need nothing more than some clean shallow trays to place the food on (old wooden window screens work well) and some cheesecloth to cover the produce and to keep out insects. To hasten sun drying of produce, you can utilize a solar dryer such as the homemade one shown above. This dryer is made by utilizing an old storm window to provide the glass, which creates the solar heat —an excellent way of recycling old storm windows back into use.

For oven drying, you will need only shallow trays and a gas or electric kitchen oven. Or to make drying more efficient, you can make the dryer as shown below which fits in the oven or on top of the

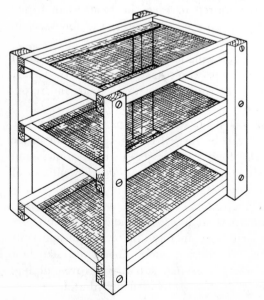

Oven dryer.

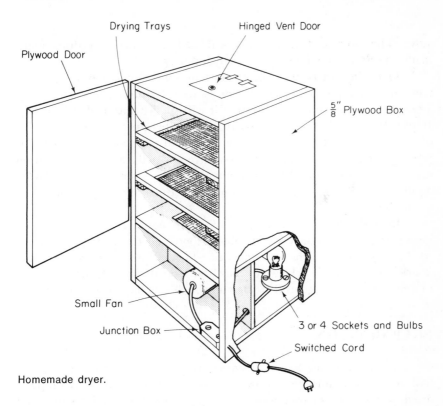

Plywood Door

Drying Trays

Hinged Vent Door

$\frac{5}{8}''$ Plywood Box

Small Fan

Junction Box

3 or 4 Sockets and Bulbs

Switched Cord

Homemade dryer.

A commercially made dryer. (*Courtesy S. W. Jay Co., West Bountiful, Utah*)

159

stove. The most consistently successful method of drying utilizes home-made dryers or purchased food dehydrators.

In drying, there must be a constant source of the proper drying temperature, and good air circulation as well. If you dry food at too low a temperature, there is a chance that it will spoil before it drys properly. If you dry it too fast and at too high a temperature, it will lose a lot of vitamins. The temperature and amount of time needed for particular produce, as well as size and thickness of food dried, can come only from experience. After you have experimented with your particular drying equipment and method, you can adjust the time and temperature a bit so the food is properly dried.

In addition to these various pieces of equipment, you will also need storage containers. Closable plastic food bags for storing the various foods, as well as airtight containers in which to place the bags of food, is one method that works well. Place the food in small food bags; then place these bags in a central storage unit such as a large new garbage can.

PREPARATION

Although drying foods for storage is quite simple, there are several basic rules that must be followed to insure that the food is properly dried and stored, so that it is not only edible, but good tasting, and loses the least amount of vitamins and nutrients. Use only good produce; a small rotten apple or insect-infested piece of fruit or vegetable can cause an entire batch of dried food to become unusable. In most cases, you should pick firm, fresh produce, and dry it as soon after picking as you possibly can. (Some food like beans are best left to dry on the plant.)

Use a clean wooden surface for cutting, peeling, and cleaning the produce, and make sure you cut the pieces of produce into approximately the same size. This makes drying much easier and provides more even-textured foods. Make sure the produce is cleaned of all dirt and debris. Wash produce thoroughly, and prepare the various fruits and vegetables according to the information given in this chapter for specific produce.

Before drying, almost all produce except onions, peppers, and herbs can be "blanched." This stops the enzyme action. Most fruits may also be treated in this manner. Blanching is actually placing the produce into boiling water for a few minutes, then plunging it into cold water for one minute. A better method is to steam the food in a wire basket placed over briskly boiling water. The following chart gives the time required to blanch and steam the different fruits and vegetables.

Steaming and Blanching Timetable

Vegetables	Boiling Water	Steam
Beans, Snap	7	10
Beans, French Style	3	5
Beans, Lima	7	10
Carrots	5	8
Corn, on Cob	3	15
Peas	5	8
Pumpkin		10
Rutabagas	5	8
Turnips	5	8

Fruits	Boiling Water	Steam
Apples	7	10
Apricots		10
Peaches		8
Pears		8
Plums	2	6

In addition, some fruits will discolor quite quickly once they have been cut into. You've probably noticed how quickly a banana, apple, or peach will turn dark after it has been cut open. Although this won't hurt the taste of the fruit, either fresh or dried, it makes it less appealing. To stop the fruit from turning dark, you can use one of several methods. One of the most common methods is to simply dip the fruit pieces into an ascorbic acid mixture or a bowl of pineapple juice. Another formula to keep fruit from darkening is to drop the pieces into a saltwater bath made up of 1 tablespoon salt for each quart of water for 15 to 20 minutes. Steaming or blanching the fruits immediately after cutting will also help retard the darkening process.

One method used for many years is sulphuring. There are 2 basic methods of sulphuring. The first utilizes sodium bisulfite or sodium sulfite; either can be purchased at a drug store. Add 1 ounce of either chemical to 7 quarts of water, and let the piece of fruit stand in the solution for 30 minutes. This method is great for small quantities of food. Larger quantities are best done by using sulphur dioxide, which can also be purchased at a drug store. You'll need about a teaspoon of sulfur dioxide for each pound of fruit. Place the fruit on wooden trays, and place in a dryer if you have one. Move the dryer outside. Place the sulfur in a metal pan about 10 inches below the trays of fruit. Place the pan up off the ground to insure air space and proper combustion. Light the sulfur; then close the dryer. If you don't have a dryer, then cover the entire stack of trays with a large box or tub. This sulfur treatment is used until the fumes turn the flesh of the fruit semitranslucent with drops of juice oozing out. It normally takes from 10 to 25 minutes, depending on the size of the fruit pieces.

With the equipment assembled and the food harvested and properly prepared, you are ready to dry it, using one of the 3 methods of drying mentioned.

SUN DRYING

Requiring little in the way of expensive equipment, electricity, or other "purchased" energy, sun drying is the most natural way of drying. However, it must be done in the proper climate. An extremely hot, dry sun is required, and it will normally take about 2 to 3 days to accomplish the proper dryness, even with ideal drying weather. Sun drying is an excellent test of whether you like dried foods and want to dry them yourself. The only equipment you will need is some old window screens and cheesecloth. Wash them thoroughly, and make sure they are clean before using. Cover screens with cheesecloth; then put fruits or vegetables on the cheesecloth, spreading out the pieces so none are touching each other. Then cover with cheesecloth to keep out insects. When night comes, take the trays of produce inside to keep them from picking up nighttime moisture, and carry them back outside again late the next morning.

While the pieces are drying, stir them around from time to time to keep them from sticking to the trays and to allow them to dry evenly throughout. Larger pieces must be turned over individually, but smaller pieces can merely be stirred.

After a couple of days if the food looks dry, test by cutting into one of the pieces. If it looks dark and moist in the center, it needs more drying time. Each particular food looks somewhat different when dried properly. For instance, peas will be wrinkled and shriveled up. Corn turns somewhat transparent. Apples, apricots, and peaches look and feel like leather. Another test you can make is to place several pieces of dried food in a glass jar, and close the lid tightly. Place the jar in a cool, dark place for a couple of days; then check the jar for condensation on the inside. If there are droplets of moisture on the inside of the jar, the food will have to be dried some more. If there is no indication of moisture, the food is properly dried and can be permanently stored.

One of the problems in testing an individual piece is that they're normally not all the same size, and some of the smaller pieces may be drier than the larger pieces. You may have to remove some of the smaller pieces and allow the larger pieces to dry longer. This is why it is so important to try to get all pieces approximately the same size for each dryer load. Also, each piece that is dry should be removed from the dryer immediately.

Although almost any food can be dried by the sun, there are some that are easier to dry than others. For instance, apples, plums, cherries, peaches, apricots, beans, and corn have been dried for centuries using solar heat.

OVEN DRYING

Next to sun drying, oven drying is the easiest in terms of special equipment needed. The trays for drying should be wooden and covered with thin cotton material. To help prevent food from sticking, cover the material with a thin coating of salad oil. Set the oven at 150°F, and allow it to warm up. Place the trays of food in the oven, and leave the door open a bit. About every half hour, move the food trays around so all will be dried evenly. Normally this means you should move the top trays down to the bottom shelf and the bottom trays up to the top shelf, and move the middle trays to the outside, etc. If you're using a gas oven, watch the oven carefully to make sure the flame doesn't go out. If you're using an electric oven, remove the top unit. Place the thermostat at 200°F to warm up; then turn it back down to 150°F.

Again, to make your drying more efficient, you can also make an oven dryer as shown on page 158 to use in your oven, rather than using the normal oven trays. You can also make a top-of-the-stove dryer as shown on page 164 and use it on top of your gas, electric, or wood-burning stove, over a heat register, or any place where there is a steady temperature of 100°F to 150°F and good air circulation. The only problem with this type of dryer is that it is not much faster than sun drying, and you are very limited in the amount of produce you can dry at one time.

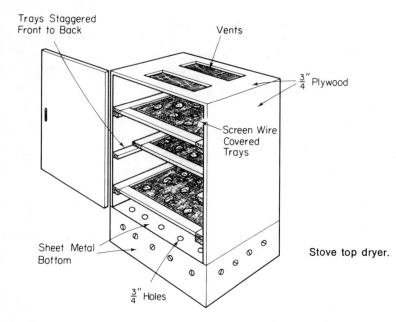

Trays Staggered
Front to Back

Vents

$\frac{3}{4}''$ Plywood

Screen Wire
Covered
Trays

Sheet Metal
Bottom

$\frac{3}{4}''$ Holes

Stove top dryer.

DEHYDRATORS

Although these are not as economical as sun drying, dryers or dehydrators not only speed up drying time but allow you to more readily utilize all of a single harvest that you might not be able to use with slower drying methods. There are several home dryers on the market today, and you can also make your own dryer if you are somewhat handy with tools. If you purchase a dryer, make sure it is of good quality. It should have plenty of trays and a good amount of air circulation around the trays. The temperature control of most purchased dryers will range from 95°F to 150°F.

If you would like to experiment with drying or would like to dry only small amounts of food inexpensively, perhaps a cardboard box dryer would be best. These are made from a cardboard box that is merely lined with foil, with a 60-watt light bulb added to the bottom. The drying tray is merely a cookie sheet that fits the top of the box. If you prefer a more sophisticated dryer, construct the one shown on page 165. This dryer has electric heat and a thermostat control. It should cost about $25 to $30 to build, depending on local prices.

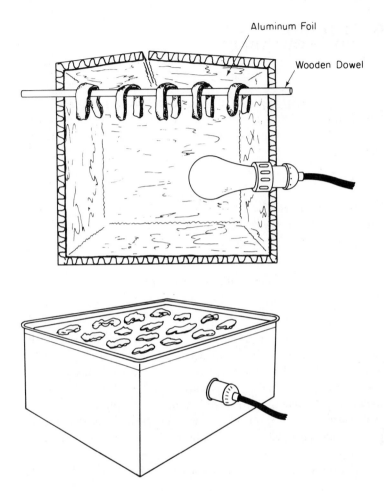

Aluminum Foil

Wooden Dowel

Box dryer.

AIR DRYING

This type of drying differs from sun drying in that it is usually done indoors in a well-ventilated room or a screened-in porch. Herbs and greens, for instance, should be air- or oven-dried to protect the color. Leather britches and strings of hot peppers are 2 of the most common air-dried items; however, other possibilities are listed with the instructions for drying. It takes longer to dry by the air-dry method, than the other forms of drying.

DRYING, STORING, AND USING
FRUITS AND VEGETABLES

Apples

Wash, peel, and core crisp apples. Quarter, slice, dice, or cut into rings. Place on trays, and dry. You can also run a string through the center of apple rings and hang to air dry. Dried apples should be "leathery" and not hard.

Apricots

Wash, halve, and pit; do not peel. Place cut-side up on drying surfaces, and dry until fruit is "leathery."

Bananas

Peel and thinly slice ripe bananas. Place slices on racks, and dry.

Beans

If the weather is dry, beans can be left on the plants and allowed to dry right in the garden. However, if the weather turns wet, the beans could mold or mildew in the pods, or they could sprout in the pods. A much more reliable method with beans is to pull the plants up by the roots when the beans have turned yellow, and hang them, plant and all, in the shade to finish drying. Shell when dry, and heat in a 180°F oven for 15 minutes; then turn off oven, and leave beans in oven 1 hour to prevent bug infestations. Green beans and yellow wax beans make good shelled beans. Beans can also be picked when yellow, the pods put on

Green beans, cut in the french style with the cutter, dry and cook much faster than whole beans.

Leather britches are whole green beans air dried on a string.

the drying trays, dried, then shelled, and stored. Or, they can be picked and shelled green and then dried on the screens. However, the dried pods are much easier to shell. Merely place pods, or plants with pods, in a cloth bag, and tramp until beans are shelled; then remove beans from the bottom of the bag. Green snap beans can be strung whole on heavy thread or strung and hung in any well-ventilated room to dry. These are commonly called "leather britches." Snap beans can also be dried whole, chopped, or cut as french-style beans and dried on trays. Leather britches are brittle when dry; snap beans are "leathery."

Beets

Wash young beets, being sure to leave root end and at least an inch of the stems intact to prevent bleeding. Cook until tender. Slip skins, and slice thinly or dice into small cubes. Dry until brittle.

Blackberries

Wash and drain well. Spread on trays, and dry until no moisture remains in center.

Blueberries or Huckleberries

Wash and drain. Spread on trays, and dry.

Boysenberries

Same as Blackberries.

Cabbage

Shred cabbage, or cut it in long, thin slices, and dry. It should be brittle when dry.

Carrots

Scrub carrots with a brush, and remove ends. Cut into ⅛ inch slices, and dry. Carrot slices can also be cooked until tender and then dried. When dry, they will be hard and brittle.

Celery

See Herbs.

Cherries

Wash and pit fully ripe cherries. Drain, saving juice for jelly or for drinking. Spread on trays to dry. They should be tough and leathery, not brittle.

Corn

There are several methods of drying sweet corn. It can either be blanched for 3 to 5 minutes in boiling water, then cooled in ice water and cut from the cob, or cut directly from the cob with no blanching. Put on drying trays, and dry. Stir and separate corn often, as the kernels tend to stick together. Another old-fashioned way of drying corn is to cut the kernels from fresh sweet corn and cook the kernels until tender, adding sugar, canning salt, and fresh sweet cream. When corn is cooked, spread in drying trays, and dry. This corn recipe doesn't have to be presoaked— just cook in water or milk. When corn is dry, it will be transparent and hard.

Sweet corn can also be left in the garden to dry. When dry, pull back husks, and hang them upside down by husks until ready for use or until kernels are hard and semitransparent. Shell, grind, and use the corn as you normally use cornmeal. Field corn can also be used in this way.

There are a few other uses for dried field corn including hominy (see recipe in Chapter 1), which can be tray-dried and ground for "grits." Dried field corn can also be soaked overnight and parched in a skillet with a little fat to make a very tasty snack.

Currants

Wash and drain. Spread on trays and dry. Use as you would raisins.

Grapes

Seedless grapes can be washed, drained, and dried. Other varieties can be cut in half, seeded, then dried.

Herbs

Almost all herbs can be dried in the same way. Cut stalks with large amounts of leaves on them after the dew has dried in the morning. Put 4 or 5 stalks together to form a clump, and hang them upside down in a shaded, well-ventilated place. When leaves are dry, crumble into jars, and always keep the jars in a dark cupboard. The leaves can also be picked from the plant and dried on trays. Celery stalks do not dry well; however, the leaves can be dried as an herb.

Loganberries

Same as Blackberries.

Mushrooms

Wash young, tender mushrooms, and drain well. Slice in $\frac{1}{4}$ inch pieces, or chop fine; spread on drying trays and dry. Mushrooms should be brittle when dry.

Okra

Wash and drain fresh okra. Slice in $\frac{1}{2}$ inch pieces leaving the seeds in, and dry.

Onions

Peel onions, and chop, grind, or grate. Spread on trays to dry. Onion flakes dry quickly and can be blown away quite easily.

Parsnips

Wash and drain; then scrape, and remove ends. Slice thinly, and spread on trays to dry. Or, cook until tender, drain, and then dry on trays. The thin slices will be brittle when dry.

Peaches

Dry only fresh, juicy, perfect peaches. Wash, halve, and remove pits. Peaches can be dried in halves, quarters, or thinly sliced. Place cut-side up on drying trays, and dry. Thoroughly dry peaches will be "leathery" with no moisture in the center.

Pears

Dry only ripe, firm pears. Wash, halve, and remove cores. Dry in halves, quarters, or thin slices. Place cut-side up on trays, and dry. Pears will also be "leathery" when properly dried.

Peas

Peas can be dried in several ways, like beans. They can be picked fresh, shelled, and spread on trays to dry, or picked and dried in the pods. They can also be left in the garden to dry. Peas should be wrinkled and thoroughly dried in the center before storing.

Peppers

Hot peppers can be strung whole and hung in a well-ventilated place to dry. These can be left on the strings until used or crushed and then placed in jars for storage. Green or sweet peppers can be quartered, with the seeds removed, and strung in the same manner. Sweet peppers can also be cut in strips, rings, or diced and dried on trays. These small pieces dry very quickly.

Plums

Prune plums can be dried whole as is, or they can be blanched in boiling water for 2 minutes to kill any infestations and to crack the skin, which aids the drying. Other varieties of plums can be dried in the same manner or halved and pitted. Dry cut-side up on trays until "leathery."

Potatoes

Irish potatoes do not dry well. See Sweet Potatoes.

Pumpkin

Halve, remove seeds and stringy portion, and then skin. Cut into small cubes and cook until tender in boiling water or steam. Drain; then place on trays to dry. Pumpkin can also be cooked, then pressed through a colander. Sweetening and spices can be added to this, then spread on trays to dry. The old-fashioned way to dry pumpkin is to slice into rings, remove seeds and peel, run a string through the slices, and hang up to dry. Do not precook if using this method. Pumpkin should be "leathery" and dry throughout before storage. The dried pulp can be cut, broken, torn, or rolled up for storage.

Raspberries

Wash gently, remove stems and any faulty berries, and then drain thoroughly. Place on trays and dry until there is no moisture in the center.

Rhubarb

Wash fresh rhubarb, and peel if desired. Rhubarb will dry faster when peeled. Cut in 1 inch pieces, and spread on trays or string and hang up to dry. Dry until no moisture shows in the center.

Rinds (Lemon, Lime, Orange, and Grapefruit)

As you use these fruits throughout the abundant season, grate the colored portion of the rind onto a plate, and leave out until dry. Pack into jars, and use for flavoring during the off-season.

Soybeans

These should be dried in the garden like other beans. Dried soybeans can be toasted in the oven and eaten as a snack like peanuts. They are good plain or with salt or other flavoring added.

Spinach, Swiss Chard (and other Greens)

Pick over fresh greens; wash and drain thoroughly. Chop coarsely into uniform pieces, and spread on trays to dry. Stir often, as these will mat together.

Dried strawberries are a welcome treat on cereal in the winter.

Squash

Summer squash should be thinly sliced and spread on trays to dry. Leave peeling on tender, young squash. Winter squash should be treated as pumpkin.

Strawberries

Wash gently; remove stems and any faulty berries. Dry whole, cut in half, or slice. Strawberries can be dried whole with the stems left on for an attractive confection, or they can be mixed with sugar or honey and spread on trays to dry. Stir often for even drying.

Sweet Potatoes

Thoroughly scrub whole sweet potatoes, pare, and slice thinly. Dry on trays until "leathery."

Tomatoes

Scald tomatoes to slip skins; then core. Slice, dice, halve, or quarter tomatoes, and drain an hour or more. Spread on drying trays, and dry. Watch trays for an accumulation of excess moisture. Tomatoes can also be pressed through a colander and the pulp (use thin juice for other vegetables, and dry only the squeezed pulp) spread on trays to dry, or the juice can be cooked on top of the stove until thicker and then spread on trays to dry.

Turnips

Wash, drain, remove ends, and slice thinly. Spread on trays to dry, or precook and then spread to dry. Turnips can also be cooked and mashed, then spread on trays to dry.

DRYING AND STORING FRUIT LEATHERS, EGGS, AND MILK

Fruit Leathers

Leathers can be made from almost any fruit, either separately, or combined with some of your favorites, and dried together. Wash, peel, and pit or core fruits. Cook in their own juices or in a very small amount of water until tender; then press through colander, and spread on trays to dry. If you wish to retain the skins for nutrition's sake, simply halve, pit, or core the fruit, and blend to a puree. Spread and dry. If the fruits aren't sweet enough for your taste, honey or sugar and spices can be added to the puree before drying. But remember, the dried fruit will be concentrated and therefore sweeter tasting than the puree. The spices will also be concentrated, so use sparingly. When properly dried, fruit leathers will be "leathery," chewy, and pliable. To store, cut leather into strips or pieces, or roll up, and place into jars. Before rolling, granulated sugar or powdered sugar can be sprinkled on top.

Left, to make fruit leather, spread strained fruit pulp in a thin layer on a cookie sheet. *Right,* when properly dried, fruit leathers will be pliable and leathery, and can be rolled up for storage.

Eggs

Eggs can be dried with either the white and yolk together or the whites and yolks separated. Beat whole eggs or yolks until light. Spread in thin layer on trays, and dry. Egg whites are gently stirred, then spread in a thin layer, and dried. An oven or indoor dryer works best for the eggs. When dried, eggs should be ground to a fine powder and stored in jars. One whole egg equals 2 tablespoons powder plus 2½ tablespoons warm water. Beat until smooth. One yolk equals 1½ tablespoons powder plus 1 tablespoon warm water. One average egg white equals 1 tablespoon powder plus 2 tablespoons warm water.

Milk

Pour fresh milk into the top of a double boiler, and simmer until most of the water has evaporated and the milk is as thick as cream. Pour thickened milk into drying trays and dry in an oven or other indoor dryer. When dry, grind to a powder, and store in jars. One part milk powder to 4 parts water will reconstitute the milk.

Meats

See Chapter 8 on Smoking, Curing, and Drying Meat.

STORAGE

In the olden days, dried food was merely placed in cloth bags and hung on nails from the rafters. But this old method isn't quite as good as it sounds. Insects can readily get at the food, as well as acrobatic mice, moisture in the air, and dirt. Dried food can be stored in glass jars, metal tins, plastic food bags, and even plastic freezer containers. Remember that the container must have a tight-fitting lid. The storage container should also keep out the light, so if you are using transparent containers, store them in a dark place. Another good idea is to use small containers such as plastic bags inside a larger varmint-proof container. Dried fruit can also be stored in airtight containers with sugar sprinkled between the layers of fruit. After filling containers, place in a cool, dry place. Before permanently storing your dried produce away for the winter months, place them in a cool, dark place where they can be checked daily for 10 to 14 days. If all is well at the end of that time, they can be stored permanently. If properly dried, the food should remain edible and nutritive for more than a year. Using transparent containers such as glass enables you to occasionally check the dried food for insects or any moisture condensing on the inside of the glass. Moisture and insects are the most common problems with dried food and are the two things you really have to watch out for. At the first sign of moisture in your stored dried produce, redry in a 300°F oven for 20 to 25 minutes.

RECONSTITUTING DRIED FOODS

Using dried foods for cooking is simple—you merely put back the water removed from the food. All dried foods except greens should be placed in water before cooking. Place the food in only enough boiling water to cover the food, and allow to soak. Most food will take up more than two times its volume in water, and if it absorbs all the water before the soaking time is up, add more water. The time required for soaking varies with each individual dried food, according to how dry the food is. Fruits normally require from 1 to 5 hours; vegetables will require less, although beans and corn may require soaking overnight. The food should be cooked in the same water it has been soaked in to preserve all the flavor as well as the vitamins and nutrients. Cover the pan while cooking, as the steam also helps "rehydrate" the food. The following information on reconstituting and cooking the various dried foods should help you get started.

COOKING WITH DRIED FRUITS
AND VEGETABLES

Fruits. Dried fruits should be soaked overnight in water. However, the fruit can be cooked without presoaking by simmering gently for about 2 hours. Cooked fruits can be eaten when tender as is or sweetened or used in pies, puddings, or other recipes calling for a specific pie filling. Fruit that has been soaked overnight and not cooked can be used in cakes, breads, muffins, cookies, and pancake batters.

Currants, raisins, bananas, and the different dried rinds can be used as is in your favorite recipes.

Currants, raisins, bananas, and strawberries are old favorites to mix dried with your favorite granola recipe. Other dried fruits can also be used with granola by grinding them or chopping fine for easier eating. Fruits can be soaked overnight and then placed on top of cold or hot cereal for a morning treat.

Blueberries can be used as is or soaked overnight for those early morning treats of muffins and pancakes.

Soaked bananas have to be used as mashed bananas for cakes, breads, or cookies.

Berries should be covered with twice their volume of cold water and then simmered gently for use in pies and other desserts.

To make fruit cake, sweeten and dry the fruits called for in your favorite fruit cake recipe and have them ready for holiday baking. Simmer the fruit in equal parts of sugar and water until transparent; drain well, and spread on trays to dry. Rinds can also be candied and dried.

Fruit leathers can be eaten as is for a nutritious dessert or snack, or they can be soaked for a few hours in water and rolled up in your favorite strudel dough. Leathers can also be simmered and eaten as stewed fruits, sweetened for a dessert topping or sauce, or used to flavor gelatin.

Rhubarb should be soaked for several hours and then simmered and sweetened for sauce or pies.

Vegetables. Dried sweet corn should be soaked for about 2 hours in water or milk. Simmer until tender adding salt, pepper, butter, or honey to taste. The dried-on-the-cob sweet or field corn is ground and used in any recipe calling for cornmeal.

Fresh parsley can be used when soaked overnight in cold water. It can also be used dried along with other herbs in cooked dishes. Many of the dried herbs make excellent teas.

Summer squash can be soaked for a few hours, dipped in batter, and fried just as you did in the summer. Winter squash is soaked, simmered and mashed, and then flavored as you normally would for winter squash. The slices of summer squash and chunks of winter squash can be used in any of your favorite recipes after presoaking.

Pumpkin for pie or bread is soaked in the refrigerator overnight in milk. Allow 1½ cups milk and ½ cup dried pumpkin for 1 pie. Adjust the amounts to fit the amounts called for in your bread recipe or to make several pies.

Other vegetables such as beets, carrots, okra, parsnips, sweet potatoes, and turnips can be soaked for an hour or two, simmered until tender, and flavored with salt, pepper, and butter. These vegetables can also be soaked and used in any number of recipes—candied carrots, carrots in cheese sauce, harvard beets, fried okra, mashed turnips, candied sweet potatoes. Of course, any variety can be combined for soups and stews. Cabbage can be simmered with butter, salt, and pepper or added to the soup or stew pot.

Dried french-cut green beans require only an hour or so of soaking and, again, can be used in any number of recipes from Green Beans Parmesan to a simple side dish flavored only with salt and pepper. Snap beans dried either whole or in 1- to 2-inch pieces require longer soaking and can be used in any recipe. Leather britches require overnight soaking and make an excellent main dish simmered with a ham bone. If leather britches are left hanging in the open air and not stored in jars, they could become quite dirty and should be washed before using. You might also want to throw out the soak water to make sure all dirt is removed.

Beans and peas you have dried yourself are cooked in the same ways as the ones from the store. Soak them overnight, or bring pot to a boil, turn off heat, and let set for 1 hour. Simmer gently until tender. Dried and shelled green and yellow wax beans cook faster than some other dried beans and make excellent baked beans. Dried peas require only a few hours of soaking and become tender much faster than beans.

Peas and beans along with any dried vegetable and meat can be made into vegetable soup without presoaking. Simmering for several hours takes the place of presoaking.

Dried onion flakes and chopped green peppers can be used in any cooked dish calling for fresh peppers and onions. Dried hot peppers can be crumbled and used in anything you want "hot," sprinkled over a pizza, or added to your own taco sauce.

Dried tomato chunks and halves, etc., can be put in any cooked recipe straight from the jar if you don't wish to add liquid to your recipe. Or they can be covered with water and presoaked to use as canned tomatoes. The dried tomato pulp is usually stirred into boiling water until dissolved, but again, small amounts could be added directly to soups, beans, etc., with no presoaking. When reconstituting the tomato pulp, make the paste as thick or as thin as you like by varying the amount of water.

Dried greens are merely put on to cook in water to cover and are simmered gently. Greens and spinach can be cooked for a short amount of time and then used in cooked recipes calling for fresh or frozen chopped spinach.

Dried mushrooms should be soaked for a few hours in cold water and can be used in almost any recipe calling for mushrooms. Mushrooms along with most other fruits and vegetables can be added to soups and stews or other long-cooking recipes without any presoaking.

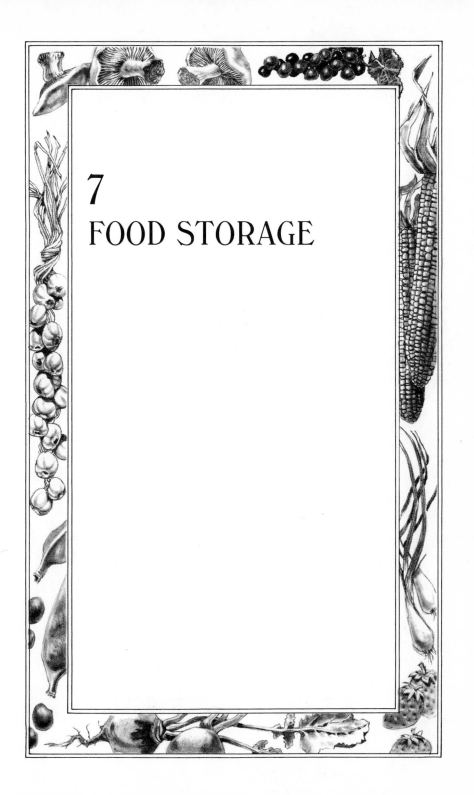

7
FOOD STORAGE

Our grandparents and great-grandparents didn't have freezers, refrigerators, and many of the other conveniences we take for granted, but they still managed to provide plenty of good eating even during the winter when they couldn't get fresh vegetables from their garden. The secret: old-fashioned things such as the root cellar and apple barrel. These old-time storage methods are as great today as they were yesterday and are still the best method of storing some fruits and vegetables, not to mention a surplus of some foods such as apples, when it just wouldn't be practical to freeze or can all the food. The best part is that storing food in this manner is the easiest and least complicated method of food preservation.

There are three basic methods of simple food storage: garden storage, barrel or pit storage, and cellar or basement storage. There are also three different types of storage conditions needed by different varieties of vegetables and fruits: cool-moist, cool-dry, and warm-dry. If you really want to store all foods properly, it would be best to have a storage area fitting these requirements for the different foods. For instance, pumpkins and winter squash do best when stored in a warm-dry area. On the other hand, potatoes and turnips do best in a cool-moist place. You can provide separate storage areas for all three, or you can incorporate the three areas in one storage, although this is a bit harder to do.

GARDEN STORAGE

In some portions of the country, a lot of vegetables are best simply left in the garden, and dug whenever needed. Brussels sprouts, leeks, salsify, parsnips, collards, and kale will withstand cold quite easily, and they can be left in the ground through the winter in all but extreme climates. Merely dig or pick out what you need, as you need them. A protective covering of about 4 inches of hay or straw mulch not only protects the vegetables, but will also make it easier for you to dig when the ground is frozen. Broccoli, spinach, cauliflower, lettuce, and Chinese cabbage will all survive frost and early winter if they are covered with a mulch of straw. If your climate is very harsh, you may wish to cover the straw mulch with a tarp or piece of plastic. One unusual vegetable, Jerusalem artichokes, actually won't store well, and is best left in the ground throughout the winter.

BARREL OR PIT STORAGE

For many years, my father has been storing surplus apples in an old-fashioned apple barrel, and when you remove the lid for apples, the pleasant heady smell of apples is an aroma you won't forget. This old-fashioned method of food storage is as easy and effective today as it was a century ago.

To make up an old-fashioned apple barrel, you'll need a good tight, solid, wooden barrel. Dig a hole about ⅔ the depth of the barrel and about a foot larger all around. Place a layer of small rocks or gravel in the bottom of the hole; then put the barrel in place. Shovel the gravel around the sides of the barrel up to ground level. Then use soil to mound up around the sides of the barrel to the top, tamping it securely in place. Fill the barrel with good sound apples. Remember that this is the origin of the saying, "One rotten apple spoils the whole barrel." Make sure the fruit has no worm holes or bruises. Very carefully lay a layer of apples in place, and follow with another layer until the barrel is full. When the barrel is full of apples, place a wire screen over the top. Then cover the entire mound and barrel with about 6 inches of old hay.

Apple barrel.

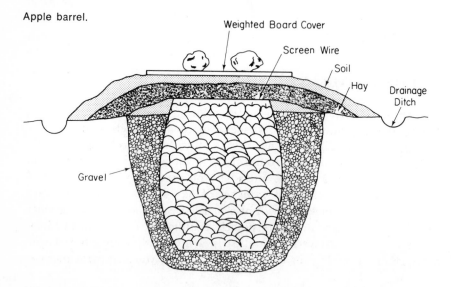

Lay a board over the hay covering the top of the barrel, weight it down with a stone, and place a 4 inch layer of soil over the hay. You may also wish to dig a drainage ditch around the barrel to allow rainwater to escape rather than to soak into the barrel. The barrel is an excellent storage place for apples and other similar fruit, but it can also be used to store potatoes, beets, carrots, salsify, turnips, and cabbage.

One of the problems with storing produce in the barrel is that when the barrel is opened, it should be emptied. A solution is to store the produce in pits, and have several small pits rather than 1 large storage pit or barrel. Another reason is that you shouldn't mix fruit and vegetables in the same barrels or pits. Different vegetables in the same pit should be separated by placing a layer of straw between them. The pits are pyramid-shaped and can be used for storing apples and pears or anything from potatoes, carrots, and cabbage to beets, turnips, and parsnips. The most efficient pits are those holding no more than a couple bushels of vegetables.

To build the pit, place a 6 inch layer of straw on the ground about 4 feet in diameter. Place the vegetables on the straw, mounding them up into a pyramid shape. *Again, don't place vegetables and fruits in the same pit.* Cover the produce with more straw, about 6 inches thick. Then shovel soil over the entire mound until it is about 4 inches thick. Using the back of a shovel, tamp the soil firmly around the mound. To provide ventilation, place a center core of straw up through the layer of soil; then cover it with a board and a stone. If you wish to ventilate a larger pit, run a couple of stakes up through the center of the mound to form a core or "flue." Then make an angled roof over the flue to keep out rainwater. The last step is to dig a drainage ditch around the entire mound to allow water to quickly escape.

The pits should be constructed in different locations each year

Cone-shaped pit.

because the leftover fruits will be rotten or insect-damaged and can cause damage to fresh produce stored the following year.

One of the problems with pits is that it is somewhat hard to dig produce out of them when the ground is frozen solid. Also, all produce has to be removed when the pit is opened.

ROOT CELLARS

The most popular method of storing produce is in an old-fashioned root cellar, and you will find that even today, those old cellars are sophisticated in design and are capable of keeping produce through the winter months. There are basically two types of root cellars: basement cellars and outdoor cellars. Basement cellars are not quite as efficient as the outdoor cellars, because it is normally harder to regulate the temperature and to keep them cool and moist enough.

Although you might be able to keep a few vegetables for a short time by merely stacking them in a corner of your basement, to really provide the proper storage, you should modify your basement to properly store your produce. If at all possible, build a special room on either the north or east corner of the basement. Partition and insulate it well from the rest of the basement. The ideal temperature should stay at around 50°F to 55°F. There should be no heating ducts from the furnace running through the room, and make sure there are also no hot water pipes running through the room. However, if it isn't possible to build the room without some heating ducts running through it, make sure they are well insulated. You need at least one window in the room for ventilation, and two is even better. The windows should be opened for ventilation but shaded to keep out light by constructing some sort of ventilator duct as shown.

The room should be at least 6 feet by 6 feet in size, and a somewhat larger room would be even better. Make sure you can close the room off securely and that the door fits snugly. Place 4-inch Fiberglas insulation in the walls, and cover with fiberboard on both sides. Cover the ceiling as well.

Ideally the cellar floor should be dirt to help keep the humidity right; however, most newer houses won't be equipped in this manner. One answer is to build wooden deck boards or slats of 2 x 4s, and occasionally sprinkle the concrete floor underneath to keep it damp but never thoroughly wet.

Many folks have discovered that the quickest and easiest method

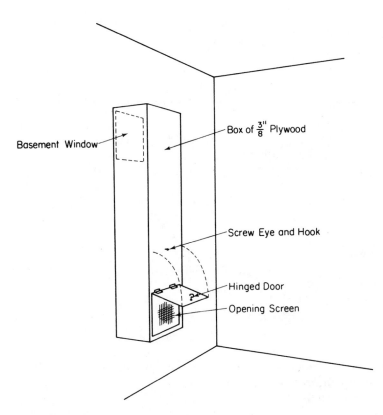

Basement Window

Box of $\frac{3''}{8}$ Plywood

Screw Eye and Hook

Hinged Door

Opening Screen

Ventilation duct.

of obtaining a good cold storage room is to buy a sauna kit and to install it in one corner of the basement. Of course you won't need the heating element, but the rest of the sauna works perfectly for storing root crops.

If at all possible, it might be wise to have a basement cellar, and even a bit of storage space next to the furnace, in addition to an outdoor root cellar. Each would provide a different atmosphere and storage for specific produce.

The old-fashioned outdoor root cellar was once a common sight in America, not only in rural areas but in the small towns and cities as well. I can well remember as a kid riding my tricycle down the sides of my grandfather's root cellar, or playing hide-and-seek and shouting down the ventilation pipe to someone else hiding in the cellar. We often waited out a summer thunderstorm or lightning storm in the cellar.

The construction of outdoor root cellars hasn't changed much even in today's time as shown above although they are quite a bit more

Outdoor cellar.

sophisticated. The important thing about outdoor underground cellars is that the temperature and humidity are more desirable and easier to regulate year-round for keeping more produce. These cellars may be attached to your house, or unattached, whichever you prefer. The best cellars are made of reinforced-poured concrete, as they were many years ago; however, they can be made of concrete block covered with concrete or a waterproofing vapor barrier. The main thing is that the roof must be solid enough to support the weight of the soil that is heaped over it. Normally the entire structure is covered with soil except for the door as shown in the illustration above. Your local State Extension Service or County Extension Agent should be able to provide you with a complete plan for building a good safe cellar.

Another important factor in building a good root cellar is to provide plenty of air circulation in order to keep the proper temperature and humidity or moisture needed. Air circulation is provided by the ventilator on top of the unit and by opening or closing the cellar door. To regulate the temperature, you will need two thermometers, preferably recording thermometers. Place one inside the cellar and one outside. You can regulate the temperature by opening or closing the ventilator on top or by opening or closing the cellar door. It takes an outside temperature well below freezing to keep the inside of the cellar at just above 32°F. Early in the morning when the temperature starts rising, close all ventilators and doors to keep the air inside cold and moist. In most areas, you will need to check the cellar daily to insure the proper temperature. Another problem is over-ventilating during freezing weather, which will result in freezing the produce, so watch carefully for this as well.

The third thing to watch carefully in a root cellar is the humidity. The chart on page 189 shows the approximate humidity at which various crops store best. If you have an old-time cellar, or build a new one, it should naturally have a dirt floor.

Most root crops will shrivel up and become useless unless they are kept in a moist atmosphere. By occasionally sprinkling water on the dirt floor, you can keep the humidity high. This will also work for a concrete floor but is not as effective. You can also cover the floor with damp straw, sawdust, or other materials. Probably the best method of preventing shriveling is to place the root crops in polyethylene bags that are punched with a few holes. Then tie the bags shut, and place these bags in wooden slat boxes.

Another important thing is to keep the cellar clean. Remove any shriveled or rotten produce as soon as possible, and have a spring house-cleaning, taking all containers and shelves, etc., outside to air out. Hose them down, and let them sun dry to remove mildew, etc. It is a good

An old-fashioned outdoor cellar is the best place to store produce.

idea to hose down the ceiling and sides of the cellar, and then apply a good coating of whitewash at the same time.

STORAGE CONTAINERS

The containers in which you store produce are also important. One of the most practical is the old-fashioned orange crate or wooden slat box. These can be used for storing everything from onions to apples. You can make these as shown below if you can't purchase or salvage them. Other good containers to use are wooden barrels or baskets and even wooden bins. Be sure to use wooden strips between the containers when stacking. This provides more air circulation. Some galvanized metal tins can be used for storing produce such as nuts, etc. Mesh bags are great for storing onions and even potatoes. Regardless of what you use, the containers should be kept at least 4 inches off the floor. Each fruit and vegetable requires somewhat different methods of preparation for storage, as well as different storage methods, temperature, and humidity. The approximate temperature and humidity should be maintained to store the various fruits and vegetables properly. This can often be maintained by separating the storage room into different compartments or by placing produce requiring more heat high on the wall and others down closer to the damp, cool floor. The following chart gives ideal situations, although you may have to adapt your particular storage situation to suit.

Storage containers.

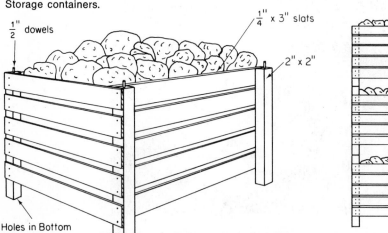

Freezing Points, Recommended Storage Conditions, and Length of Storage Periods of Vegetables and Fruits

Commodity	Freezing point	Place to store	Storage conditions		Length of storage period
	°F.		Temperature °F.	Humidity	
Vegetables:					
Dry beans and peas		Any cool, dry place	32° to 40°	Dry	As long as desired.
Late cabbage	30.4	Pit, trench, or outdoor cellar.	Near 32° as possible	Moderately moist.	Through late fall and winter.
Cauliflower	30.3	Storage cellar	do.	do.	6 to 8 weeks.
Late celery	31.6	Pit or trench; roots in soil in storage cellar.	do.	do.	Through late fall and winter.
Endive	31.9	Roots in soil in storage cellar.	do.	do.	2 to 3 months.
Onions	30.6	Any cool, dry place	do.	Dry	Through fall and winter.
Parsnips	30.4	Where they grew, or in storage cellar.	do.	Moist	Do.
Peppers	30.7	Unheated basement or room	45° to 50°	Moderately moist.	2 to 3 weeks.
Potatoes	30.9	Pit or in storage cellar	35° to 40°	do.	Through fall and winter.
Pumpkins and squashes	30.5	Home cellar or basement	55°	Moderately dry.	Do.
Root crops (miscellaneous)		Pit or in storage cellar	Near 32° as possible	Moist	Do.
Sweetpotatoes	29.7	Home cellar or basement	55° to 60°	Moderately dry.	Do.
Tomatoes (mature green).	31.0	do.	55° to 70°	do.	4 to 6 weeks.
Fruits:					
Apples	29.0	Fruit storage cellar	Near 32° as possible	Moderately moist.	Through fall and winter.
Grapefruit	29.8	do.	do.	do.	4 to 6 weeks.
Grapes	28.1	do.	do.	do.	1 to 2 months.
Oranges	30.5	do.	do.	do.	4 to 6 weeks.
Pears	29.2	do.	do.	do.	See text.

One common old wives' tale about storing fruits and apples is that they should be waxed. This is commonly used for commercial storage, mainly to give the produce a better appearance and protection during shipping, but it is not necessary for home food storage.

Two main rules are that produce should be handled carefully so it won't be bruised, and only good produce, free of blemishes and insect infestation, should be stored. When harvesting, make sure the containers you use don't have sharp wire edges or staples that will cut or scratch the produce. You should also harvest the produce in the early morning if possible, so it won't have very much field heat. Or you can let fruits and vegetables cool outdoors overnight before storing.

The best produce for storing are those that are especially bred for storage. They should be a late crop variety so that they won't be overly ripe at the time of storage. Another reason for late crops is that the harvest should be as late in the year as possible so that you won't have too long a storage period while the weather is still warm. All vegetables should be harvested with about an inch of the top or stem left in place. This prevents the produce from bleeding and losing nutrients. It also prevents the possibility of a scar on the vegetable, which could start decay.

Although it is suggested by some that the produce should be washed or brushed before storage, this only provides more opportunity for bruising or cutting the produce, and the best method believed by most old-timers is to merely shake as much soil and debris off as possible, then store. Again, don't store fruits and vegetables together. The gas produced by apples can cause potatoes to sprout, while cabbage and turnips can give their odors to apples. The solution is to place each on opposite sides of the room, and separate as much as possible. Another method of preventing this is to wrap each apple and pear in a piece of paper.

Again, as each fruit or vegetable requires different methods, here's "how" for the individual fruits and vegetables.

STORING FRUITS AND VEGETABLES

Apples

Most fruits require a somewhat lower temperature, and apples store best and for longer periods at somewhere around 32°F. Naturally, the best method of storing them winter-long is in apple barrels or pits, although you can store them for shorter periods in a basement cellar or outdoor cellar. Choose varieties that are good keepers such as Winesap, York

Imperial, Yellow Northern Spy, Newton, Arkansas Baldwin, and Black
Twig. Although apples keep better at cool temperatures, they shouldn't
be allowed to freeze.

Pick only those apples that are mature and hard, and make sure
that there are no bruises or insect infestations. Don't store apples that
have "water core" or glassy spots in the flesh. You will also need a
moderate amount of moisture to keep apples. Placing them in wooden
boxes lined with perforated polyethylene bags is one good method. But
don't seal or close the bags, or there will be too much moisture created,
and the apples will rot. Apples store best when cooled quickly by frosty
fall air and kept at about 32°F.

Cabbage

Cabbage is best stored out in a pit, although it can be stored in an
outdoor root cellar. Some folks store cabbages successfully in root cellars
by storing them root-end up in clean, dry hay. They should not be stored

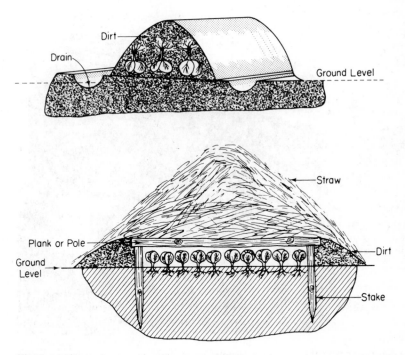

Cabbage pits.

indoors in a basement cellar, because the odor of cabbage will permeate the entire house. To store them in a pit, pull up leaving roots on the plant, and place them head-down in the pit; then cover with straw and soil.

Celery

Late maturing celery plants will keep for a couple of months in the garden. The best method is to pull the soil up around them, gradually building up the soil until it covers the plants before freezing. When the weather becomes much colder, cover with straw and weight down with a few boards. Or you can also store celery in pits or trenches. The trench should be about 12 inches wide and 24 inches deep. Place the mature plants in the trench, packing them down well. Water the plants as you place them in the trench. After the tops have dried down, cover with a board on one side and soil on the other side, making a sort of roof over the trench. Spread straw over the trench, adding more straw as the weather gets colder.

Celery can be kept in the ground if trenched and covered with boards and straw.

Celery can be stored in a cellar for a couple of months, but it shouldn't be stored in the same cellar with turnips or cabbage, or it will pick up these flavors. To store in a cellar, dig plants just before freezing weather, leaving the soil around the root clump, and place root-down on the cellar floors. Pack down tightly, and keep moist.

You can also store celery in a hotbed by merely substituting the glass cover with boards or tarpaper, packing the celery in the hotbed the same as you would in a trench or pit.

Citrus Fruits

It is to your advantage to purchase wholesale lots of citrus fruits, and store them in the root cellar. They can be kept for several weeks if the temperature is kept about 32°F, but not freezing. They should be stored up off the floor to prevent mildew.

Endive

Endive may be stored in a cellar, in much the same manner as celery, for 2 to 3 months. The leaves should be tied together to help in the blanching process.

Grapes

In some parts of the country where grapes mature late in the season, some folks keep a surplus of grapes in the cellar. Grapes will not last more than a month or two and should be stored in a cold, fairly moist area. They shouldn't be stored in a room with any other fruits or vegetables, as they quickly absorb the odors. The best grapes for keeping are Catawbas.

Onions

Onions are one vegetable that shouldn't be stored in the cellar. They should be stored in a well-ventilated attic, garage, or other unheated room. Select only mature onions that are not damaged and that don't have thick necks. Another thing to remember is that onions that have been grown from sets will not keep as well. You can keep these onions by placing a single layer of onions, necks-down, over poultry netting that is suspended in a cold, dry place. The normal procedure for storing onions is to pull them when the tops fall over, and leave them on the ground for a couple of days. Then you can either tie them in long ropes

One method of storing onions is to string them and hang in kitchen or from rafters in cellar.

to hang or place them in mesh bags. Fill the bags only about half full, and hang them overhead on hooks. We like to braid a couple of strings of onions and hang them on the beams in our kitchen. Not only are they handy, but they provide an old-time look to the kitchen. Although mild freezing won't hurt onions, they shouldn't be handled while they are still frozen.

Parsnip, Horseradish, and Salsify

All of these vegetables do best merely left in the garden all winter. They should be kept covered with a heavy mulch to prevent the alternate freezing and thawing that will eventually damage them. They can, however, be stored like other root crops if you have the room.

Pears

Pears should be picked and stored in much the same manner as apples, and, in fact, they can easily be stored in the same area. The main thing is to select only good, unbruised pears and those that are good keepers. The early pears such as Bartlett or Kieffer are normally used for canning, while hardier varieties such as Anjoy, Easter Beurre, and Winter Nells can be stored.

Pick fully mature but not quite ripe pears that are still firm and green-colored. They should be ready to pick when the color changes from a dark green to a light green. Pears should be kept cool in a moist area. One of the problems with keeping pears is that they will rot before ripening if kept at a temperature over 75°F.

Peppers

Although it seems a bit of a chore for the length of time involved, you can store green peppers for about a month if you take very good care of them. The best peppers for storage are good, firm, dark green peppers. Harvest the peppers just before the first frost; then rinse and sort according to how ripe and firm they are. Line a wooden slat box with polyethylene that has holes punched in it about 3 inches apart. Place peppers in the box, and store at about 45°F to 50°F. They should be kept in a dark place.

Hot peppers are easy to store. Merely allow them to dry on the plant, or pick, string on thread, and hang to dry in loops in the attic, garage, or even in the kitchen. We like some in the kitchen along with the onions. They all add a fragrance that seems to permeate our old-fashioned kitchen. My dad pulls up the pepper plants and hangs them upside down in his garage just before the first frost, then picks them off after they have ripened and dried. Hot peppers like onions shouldn't be stored in a root cellar.

Potatoes

Potatoes are probably the most often-stored root crop and have been a tradition with our family for years. When it comes time to dig potatoes, we pull an old one-horse plow down the row, and it lays the potatoes out on top of the soil for easy harvesting. Like most vegetables, an important point in harvesting potatoes for storage is to make sure you don't cut or bruise them. Sort out any that have bad spots in them, as well as those that have green skins. The potatoes should be dug just when the vines die.

After harvesting, spread them out under a shade tree where there is plenty of air circulation but where the hot sun won't burn them. Allow them to dry for several days to set the skins. Again, the later varieties of potatoes will store better than early potatoes, because of the additional time they're stored. However, early potatoes can be left in the ground in areas where the temperature is not too high and where there isn't too much rainfall. Merely cultivate or hoe the soil up around the plants, making sure all potatoes are well-covered so they won't turn green from sunlight. Late in the summer you can dig these potatoes and store them like late potatoes. Early potatoes should be harvested at 70°F and preferably in the morning. Some folks say to cure the potatoes at about 60°F for a week. This helps heal any small cracks or skinned areas. Early potatoes should be stored in an area with a temperature of from 60°F to 75°F. At temperatures above 80°F, they will quickly spoil.

Late-season potatoes can be stored in outdoor pits and indoor cellars, but they seem to store best in outdoor cellars where they can be kept fairly moist and at a temperature somewhere between 35°F and 40°F. They should also be stored in a dark area so they won't turn green. Late potatoes should be air dried and cured just like early potatoes. To cure, keep them at about 60°F to 75°F for a couple of weeks to heal over any wounds.

One problem with potatoes is that if they are kept below 35°F for several months, the starch turns to sugar and they become sweet. To correct this, hold the potatoes at 70°F for about a week before using them. Potatoes can be stored in mesh sacks or in slatted wooden containers.

Sweet Potatoes

Sweet potatoes can be kept all winter and into late spring if they are handled and stored properly. Sweet potatoes will bruise very easily, so you have to be very careful in harvesting and storing them. It's a good idea to harvest them directly into the containers in which they will be stored. Sweet potatoes must be cured before storage. The best method is to keep them in a moist warm area for 10 days to 2 weeks. The best temperature is from 80°F to 85°F. To maintain this temperature during the curing process, place the sweet potatoes near a furnace, cookstove, chimney, or any other steady source of heat. To keep the high humidity needed, stack the boxes of sweet potatoes on top of each other, and cover with a heavy rug or blanket. If the temperature is lower, perhaps around 65°F, keep the potatoes in the area to cure for about 3 weeks. When the potatoes have cured, move them to a part of your house, perhaps a basement room with a furnace (but not near the furnace), where there is a steady temperature of 55°F to 60°F. If your house doesn't have central heat, you can still keep sweet potatoes by wrapping them in fireproof paper and placing them near a register, warm chimney, or even a stove. Sweet potatoes are quickly damaged if they are chilled below 50°F, and for this reason they shouldn't be stored outdoors in pits.

Pumpkins and Squash

Winter squash, hard rind squash, and pumpkins will keep most of the winter if properly cared for. We always grow a few winter squash, pick them just before the first frost, and keep a bowl-full on a shelf, just another addition to our kitchen full of goodies. The main idea in keeping pumpkins and squash is to harvest just before the first frost, and make sure you leave a piece of stem on the pumpkin or squash when you remove it from the plant. Like all other produce, select only good, firm, mature pumpkins and squash that don't have bruises or insects in them.

Pumpkins and squash should also be cured for about 10 days at 80°F to 85°F. A good idea is to place them near the furnace or another source of steady heat. The warm air will heal the surface and harden the rind. When cured, store in a dry area at about 55°F to 60°F. This may mean a basement room with a furnace or even an attic. You will have to find the area that is the most suitable. It should be warm and dry. If pumpkins are kept in an area below 50°F, they will become chilled and rot. If they are kept in an area above 60°F, they will quickly become dry and stringy. Pumpkins and squash should not be stored in outdoor pits because they will freeze and become useless.

Acorn squash needs a somewhat different treatment. They don't need curing before storage but should be stored in a dry place for 35 to 40 days at 45°F to 50°F. They will become orange, dry, and stringy if cured or stored at higher temperatures.

Tomatoes

Although most of us don't think of tomatoes as a root cellar crop, those last green tomatoes can be gathered just before the first hard frost and stored for a month or so while they slowly ripen. You will have tomatoes until Thanksgiving if you are careful with your storage and handling. If a hard frost catches you before you can get them, pick only those tomatoes that were not damaged by the freezing weather. Harvest tomatoes and remove stems. Wash them carefully, and allow to dry. They should not be brushed or wiped to remove soil, or they will become sand-scarred, and any bruises or tiny cuts will soon lead to decay. Sort the tomatoes according to how ripe they are, and place one layer deep in separate trays: one tray all green, another with some red showing, etc.

At 65°F to 70°F tomatoes will keep for a couple of weeks. This ripening can be slowed a bit by keeping the tomatoes colder than 55°F. However, the tomatoes should not be kept below 50°F over a couple of days. When held at 55°F, green tomatoes that are fully mature will ripen in about a month. Green tomatoes that are less mature will take a bit more time to ripen. The room for holding tomatoes should be well-ventilated and kept fairly moist. However, too much dampness will cause the tomatoes to rot, and immature ones will often shrivel up before they ripen. Tomatoes can also be individually wrapped in paper or placed in polyethylene-film bags that have been perforated to keep moisture for the proper humidity. They should be checked once a week and any shriveled or rotten tomatoes discarded; otherwise, they will affect the other tomatoes in the room.

STORING ROOT CROPS, NUTS, AND GRAINS

Root Crops

Root crops comprise several different vegetables, and many of these can be stored outdoors in pits, as well as in a root cellar. However, they are often more conveniently stored in a cellar. Root crops include such vegetables as beets, carrots, turnips, winter radishes, celeriac, kohlrabi, and rutabagas. All of these crops will stand up under heavy frost and are best left in the garden until the nights become cold enough so that the crops will store properly.

If at all possible, harvest the crops when the ground is dry, and prepare them for storage immediately. Cut off the top of the plant to leave about one or two inches above the crown. This prevents bleeding of the plant. Some folks prefer to wash the produce, while others say to store as is because you stand less chance of bruising them. Make sure that the produce is not exposed to drying winds and that it is cool when placed in storage. Most root crops will keep best at about 32°F to 40°F. They will also need a high humidity to keep them from shriveling. If they are stored at a temperature of 45°F or higher, they will become woody and start to sprout new tops. Turnips will also give off odors, so they shouldn't be stored in a basement cellar or with fruits or produce that will pick up odors. Turnips will keep in the garden much longer than most vegetables, and we keep our turnips in the garden until New Year's Day, merely covering with a heavy hay mulch and digging out what we need each time. Although turnips will withstand heavy freezing, they can't withstand alternate freezing and thawing. There are many arguments on what root crops should be stored in. Some say sawdust, others say sand, but we think beets, turnips and parsnips store best in either hay or sand, while carrots store best in sand alone. Other good materials are layers of dry or moist sand, dry sawdust, sphagnum moss, peat moss, or leaves. Some folks like to place the crops in a crate lined with polyethlyene film. Use the method that works best for you.

Nuts

While still in their shells, nuts may be kept in root cellars in mesh sacks or wooden crates. Once they have been cracked and the kernels are exposed, they should be picked out and put in the freezer. Nuts should be cured to store properly. After you hull them, dry in a cool, dark, well-ventilated place. They should be placed in wire trays and not more than two layers deep for the curing.

Grains

Although storing quantities of grains is not for everyone, folks on homesteads with a surplus of wheat, barley, or other grains and a home-grinder may be interested in how to store them properly. Grains are extremely hard to store and keep edible. One of the problems is today's method of harvesting. In olden times, wheat and other grains were cut, shocked, and left to cure in the field. Today, grain is combined with huge mechanical pickers and is still somewhat green when harvested. The best method for homesteaders is to winnow it in front of a fan to remove all chaf and wild weed seeds; then pour into clean, dry sacks, and place in a wire mesh enclosure to keep rats and mice away. The atmosphere should be at about 40°F with a relative humidity of not over 50%. Every few days, pick the bags up, turn them, and shake them to distribute the grain and dry it evenly. After it has cured for about a month to 6 weeks, pour it into clean, dry, metal drums, and keep in a dry place. Small quantities of grain can be stored in the freezer.

As you can see, some fruits and vegetables store best in an outdoor root cellar, others best in your basement, some best outdoors in pits, while some store best in the attic. The trick is to know what stores best where and to have some storage space for each, perhaps utilizing all the storage areas.

8
DRYING,
CURING,
AND SMOKING MEAT

About the only method of meat preservation the primitive people had was drying, and today this age-old method is still being used by the Northwestern Indians to preserve racks of salmon for winter months. In addition to drying, salting was also common, with salt pork one of the mainstays of early day sailing ships. Keeping a good supply of winter meat has been a problem with man for many ages, and even our great-grandparents often had to rely on brined, cured, and smoked meats as a staple diet. Today, freezing is probably the simplest method of meat storage, but a frozen pork roast will never take the place of a country cured ham.

We won't go into the complicated process of slaughtering beef, pork, etc., because that would take a book in itself. We will, however, illustrate various ways of preserving the different types of meat. The two charts showing the wholesale cuts of pork and beef are not only important in curing and preserving, but in determining good buys in meat cuts as well. (See pages 204–207.) There are plenty of good books on slaughtering that can be obtained from the Superintendent of Documents, U.S. Government Printing Office, Washington, D.C. 20402. You can also get these booklets at your local County Extension Office. Another excellent book is published by the Morton Salt Company, a division of Morton-Norwich Products, Inc., 110 North Wacker Drive, Chicago, Ill. 60606.

Remember that dried, cured, or smoked meat is not necessarily cooked meat and should not be considered as a ready-to-eat food. A country cured ham is not the same thing as a precooked picnic ham from the supermarket. To eliminate the possibility of getting trichinosis from eating raw pork, pork has to be either thoroughly cooked before eating or treated by freezing at 0°F or lower. Venison and bear meat are also susceptible to trichinosis.

CURING MEATS

One of the most universal methods of preserving meats is by curing, a practice still used to preserve and flavor hams, shoulders, and bacon. These methods have been handed down from generation to generation, and a lot of older farm families still retain their family

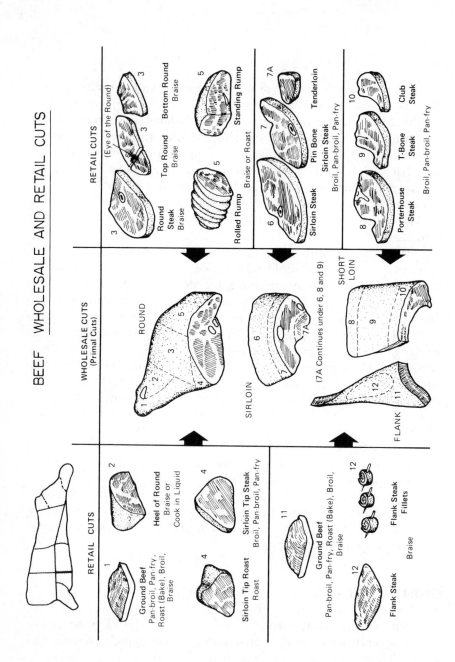

BEEF WHOLESALE AND RETAIL CUTS

RETAIL CUTS

(Eye of the Round)

3
3
3
3
Round Steak
Braise
Top Round
Braise
Bottom Round
Braise

5
Rolled Rump
Braise or Roast
5
Standing Rump

7A
Tenderloin
7
Pin Bone
Sirloin Steak
Broil, Pan-fry, Pan-fry
6
Sirloin Steak

10
Tenderloin
9
T-Bone Steak
Club Steak
8
Porterhouse Steak
Broil, Pan-broil, Pan-fry

WHOLESALE CUTS
(Primal Cuts)

ROUND
5
3
2
1
4

SIRLOIN
6
7A
7
(7A Continues under 6, 8 and 9)

SHORT LOIN
8
9
10

FLANK
12
11

RETAIL CUTS

2
Heel of Round
Braise or
Cook in Liquid

1
Ground Beef
Pan-broil, Pan-fry,
Roast (Bake), Broil,
Braise

4
Sirloin Tip Steak
Broil, Pan-broil, Pan-fry

4
Sirloin Tip Roast
Roast

11
Ground Beef
Pan-broil, Pan-fry, Roast (Bake), Broil,
Braise

12
Flank Steak
Fillets

12
Flank Steak
Braise

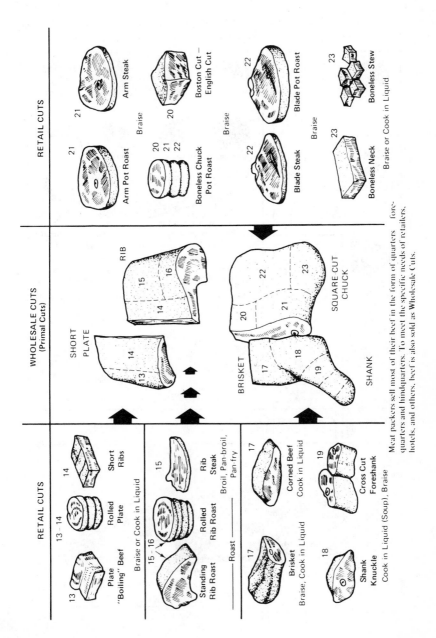

RETAIL CUTS

21 Arm Pot Roast
21 Arm Steak

Braise

20 Boston Cut —
    English Cut
20
21 Boneless Chuck
22 Pot Roast

Braise

22 Blade Pot Roast
22 Blade Steak

Braise

23 Boneless Stew
23 Boneless Neck

Braise or Cook in Liquid

WHOLESALE CUTS
(Primal Cuts)

RIB

15
16
14

SHORT
PLATE

14
13

SQUARE CUT
CHUCK

22
23
20
21

BRISKET

17
18
19

SHANK

RETAIL CUTS

13 – 14

13 Plate
    "Boiling" Beef

14 Rolled
    Plate

14 Short
    Ribs

Braise or Cook in Liquid

15 – 16

15 Standing
    Rib Roast

15 Rolled
    Rib Roast

15 Rib
    Steak

Broil, Pan-broil,
Pan-fry

——— Roast ———

17 Brisket

17 Corned Beef

Braise, Cook in Liquid   Cook in Liquid

18 Shank
    Knuckle

19 Cross Cut
    Foreshank

Cook in Liquid (Soup), Braise

Meat packers sell most of their beef in the form of quarters — fore-quarters and hindquarters. To meet the specific needs of retailers, hotels, and others, beef is also sold as Wholesale Cuts.

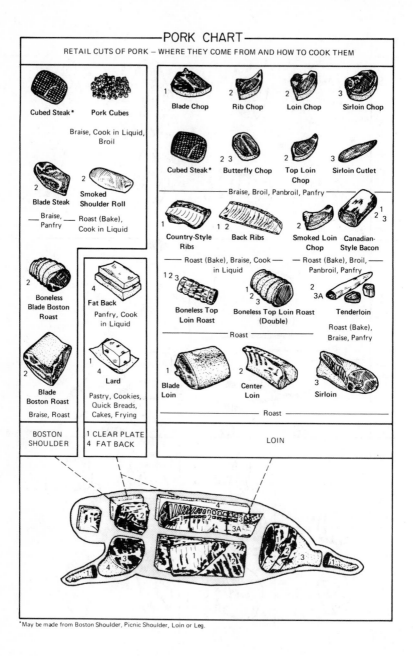

PORK CHART

RETAIL CUTS OF PORK — WHERE THEY COME FROM AND HOW TO COOK THEM

Cubed Steak * **Pork Cubes**

Braise, Cook in Liquid, Broil

Blade Chop 2 **Rib Chop** 2 **Loin Chop** 3 **Sirloin Chop**

2 3
Cubed Steak * **Butterfly Chop** 2 **Top Loin Chop** 3 **Sirloin Cutlet**

Braise, Broil, Panbroil, Panfry

Blade Steak 2

Braise, Panfry

Smoked Shoulder Roll 2

Roast (Bake), Cook in Liquid

1 **Country-Style Ribs** 1 2 **Back Ribs** 2 **Smoked Loin Chop** 1 2 3 **Canadian-Style Bacon**

Roast (Bake), Braise, Cook in Liquid

Roast (Bake), Broil, Panbroil, Panfry

Boneless Blade Boston Roast 2

Fat Back 4

Panfry, Cook in Liquid

1 2 3 **Boneless Top Loin Roast** 1 2 3 **Boneless Top Loin Roast (Double)** 2 3A **Tenderloin**

Roast

Roast (Bake), Braise, Panfry

Blade Boston Roast 2

Braise, Roast

Lard 1 4

Pastry, Cookies, Quick Breads, Cakes, Frying

1 **Blade Loin** 2 **Center Loin** 3 **Sirloin**

Roast

BOSTON SHOULDER	1 CLEAR PLATE 4 FAT BACK	LOIN

*May be made from Boston Shoulder, Picnic Shoulder, Loin or Leg.

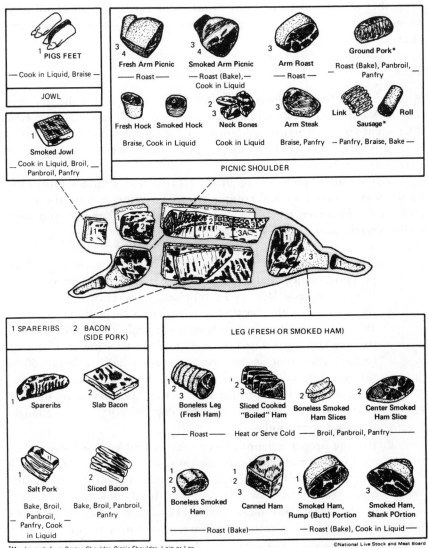

PIGS FEET

Cook in Liquid, Braise

JOWL

Smoked Jowl
Cook in Liquid, Broil, Panbroil, Panfry

Fresh Arm Picnic — Roast

Smoked Arm Picnic — Roast (Bake), Cook in Liquid

Arm Roast — Roast

Ground Pork*
Roast (Bake), Panbroil, Panfry

Fresh Hock Smoked Hock
Braise, Cook in Liquid

Neck Bones
Cook in Liquid

Arm Steak
Braise, Panfry

Link   Roll
Sausage*
Panfry, Braise, Bake

PICNIC SHOULDER

1 SPARERIBS   2 BACON (SIDE PORK)

Spareribs

Slab Bacon

Salt Pork
Bake, Broil, Panbroil, Panfry, Cook in Liquid

Sliced Bacon
Bake, Broil, Panbroil, Panfry

LEG (FRESH OR SMOKED HAM)

Boneless Leg (Fresh Ham)

Sliced Cooked "Boiled" Ham

Boneless Smoked Ham Slices

Center Smoked Ham Slice

Roast — Heat or Serve Cold — Broil, Panbroil, Panfry

Boneless Smoked Ham

Canned Ham

Smoked Ham, Rump (Butt) Portion

Smoked Ham, Shank POrtion

Roast (Bake) — Roast (Bake), Cook in Liquid

*May be made from Boston Shoulder, Picnic Shoulder, Loin or Leg.

©National Live Stock and Meat Board

This chart approved by
National Live Stock and Meat Board

recipes. If your family hasn't been curing its own meat for generations, start your own tradition. Start with one of the basic recipes; over the years that recipe will be changed to suit your needs, the spices adjusted to suit your taste, and the methods simplified to suit your taste and climate.

Pork

There are two basic methods of curing pork. One is called the *dry cure* and uses either salt, salt with sugar, or sugar with salt and saltpeter. The sugar-salt cure is the old-fashioned "sugar-cure" method which is so highly prized in gourmet shops. The second method is *liquid* or *sweet-pickle curing.*

Dry curing is preferred by many because it is simple, requires less in the way of materials and equipment, and is quicker than the sweet-pickle cure. However, regardless of which method you choose, you must follow certain basic rules to insure good, safe, edible meats.

1. The first and most important rule is that the meat must be properly chilled and kept cold during the curing process. For this reason, most folks prefer butchering and curing meat during the winter months, because it is easier to keep the meat below 40°F. Do not allow it to freeze; if the temperature drops below freezing during the curing time, add the same number of days to the curing time as the freezing weather lasts. At below 36°F, the salt will not penetrate properly. Keep a record of curing time, and try to figure the curing time as close as possible. If cured too long, the meat may become too salty; if not enough, the meat may spoil.

2. Use the proper amount of salt (not iodized salt) as indicated in each recipe, and make sure the meat is thoroughly covered with salt. If you use too little salt, the meat may spoil. If you use too much salt, the meat will become dry, hard, and too salty-tasting to eat. Weigh the meat, and make sure you have the proper amount of ingredients for the poundage of meat you're curing.

3. If you wish to smoke the meat for longer storage, make sure you follow all smoking rules properly, and smoke it long enough to dry the meat properly and reduce the moisture content.

Again, the main rule to remember is that meat must be thoroughly chilled and all animal heat gone before any curing agent is used on it.

Dry Cure Pork. Make sure meat is thoroughly chilled to below 40°F by checking internal temperature of hams near bone socket with a meat thermometer. Trim off excess fat and gristle, wipe off all blood, and weigh each piece of meat. For each 100 pounds of ham or shoulder, use:

8 pounds salt (not iodized table salt)
3 pounds brown or white sugar
2 ounces saltpeter

> *NOTE:* Some people prefer to leave out the saltpeter since it is the chemical potassium nitrate, or sodium nitrate (chile saltpeter). There are two reasons for using it: it keeps down the growth of bacteria that might be harmful, and it keeps the color of the meat red. Although there is quite a bit of controversy, it is, however, still recommended by the USDA in all their booklets on curing. Ascorbic acid is now being used to retain the red color of meat.

If you are curing bacon or other thinner cuts, use only half the above amount.

Mix all ingredients thoroughly. Divide this curing mixture into two equal parts. The meat is placed on a clean surface, and half the curing mixture is rubbed over all surfaces of the meat. A layer about ⅛ inch thick should cover the lean portion of the hams. Make sure you work the curing mixture thoroughly into the bone ends and under the skin. Place the treated meat in a clean barrel or crock, or place on a clean shelf, being careful not to knock off the curing mixture. Keep stored in a cold area from 36°F to 40°F for 2 days per pound for each ham (not total poundage). Mark the date on the calendar, and keep a good record. After about 6 to 8 days, remove the meat, and resalt with the second portion of the mixture. The curing time should be a minimum of 25 days. If curing bacon, use all the ingredients at once, and leave in the barrel rather than removing to resalt. Bacon and other smaller cuts of meat should be cured 1½ days per pound.

After curing is complete, brush the excess curing mixture from the pieces, wrap in paper and then in muslin sacks, and hang in a cold place such as an outbuilding or barn until warm weather. Or you can smoke them for longer storage as we discuss later. To prepare the meat for smoking, soak hams and shoulders for at least 2 hours in cold water, and soak bacon and smaller cuts of meat at least 30 minutes. Hang in a cold place to dry for at least a week; then proceed to smoke the meat.

Left, rub dry-cure mixture well into all sides of the meat. *Right,* pack coated meat into a crock, barrel, or place in a curing box or into a curing shelf.

Sweet-Pickle Cured Pork. The second method of curing pork is the sweet-pickle cure. Although this method requires a bit more work, it is preferred by some. Place a clean barrel or crock in a cold storage area (from 36°F to 40°F). Trim the chilled meat cuts to remove all excess fat, gristle, unwanted meat, and blood, and place the meat in a barrel or crock. Make up a cold pickle solution by dissolving 8 pounds salt, 3 pounds sugar, and 2 ounces of saltpeter into 4½ gallons of (36°F to 40°F) water. When this solution is thoroughly mixed and at the proper temperature, pour it over the meat until it covers the meat. Place a clean pan or board on top of the meat, and place a clean weight to keep the meat down in the solution. Be sure to keep the meat at the proper temperature—between 36°F and 40°F.

On the seventh day, remove the meat, pour out the curing mixture into another container, repack the meat, stir up the mixture, and pour it back over the meat. This procedure is called "overhauling" the pack. The meat should be overhauled twice more—on the 14th and 28th day.

It normally takes about 4 days per pound for hams and shoulders and a minimum of 28 days for the lighter cuts such as bacon. Although you can leave the pork in the pickle mixture until needed, it will become quite salty and is better if kept in some other manner. Remove the meat from the brine, and soak in cold water for an hour, hang in a cold place to dry, and place in smoker. If you do not wish to smoke the meat, clean the meat in water, and hang to dry for about a week. Loosely wrap the meat in paper and then in muslin, and hang in a cold place until the weather warms.

To brine cure the meat, pack the meat into a barrel or crock and cover with the cold brining solution.

If at any time during overhauling the pickling mixture becomes sour, ropy, or syrupy, discard it, scrub the meat in hot water, and scald and rechill the barrel. Place meat back in barrel, and cover with a new solution using 5½ gallons of water instead of 4½ gallons for the new solution.

You can also cure big game such as elk in the same manner.

Pumping. Pumping is a means of curing meat from the inside out and is sometimes used in conjunction with the dry or liquid cure. Pumping meat is simple and requires only a meat pump and some of the sweet-pickle cure. Fill the pump with the cure, and insert the needle along the bone on large hams. Press the plunger, withdrawing the needle at the same time. Pinch together the hole left by the needle for a few

Pumping meat.

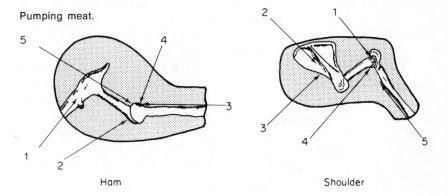

Ham   Shoulder

minutes to keep the cure from flowing back out of the hole. Insert the pump approximately 5 times along the bones of a large ham, and plan on 1 to 1½ ounces of cure for each pound of ham.

Some people feel pumping should only be used for sweet-pickle cured meat and never on sugar-cured or dry-cured meats, while others feel pumping should never be used. However, if you have had trouble with meat keeping, then it's worth a try.

Beef

Beef can be cured into two products: either corned beef or dried beef. Corned beef is usually made from the tougher, fatter cuts of beef (rump, chuck, or plate), while dried beef is usually made from the muscled cuts such as the round. Veal or calf shouldn't be used for corned beef.

Proceed as follows for both forms of beef: bone out the cuts, and cut the pieces to about the same size and thickness. Use 8 to 10 pounds of coarse, meat salt to each 100 pounds of beef. Place a layer of salt in the bottom of a sterilized crock or wooden barrel. Rub each piece of meat with salt, and pack into the barrel in layers with more salt between the layers. Top with a layer of salt. Leave undisturbed for 24 hours, and then prepare a brine of 4 pounds sugar, 2 ounces baking soda, 4 ounces saltpeter, and 4 gallons of water for each 100 pounds of meat. Pour this over the packed meat and salt, making sure it covers the meat, place a pan lid, board, or other cover over the meat, and weight it down to keep the meat down in the solution.

It will normally require from 30 to 40 days to cure the beef to good quality corned beef. It should be kept somewhere between 34°F and 38°F to cure properly. If the temperature becomes warm and the brine solution becomes ropy, remove the meat, wash it in warm water, repack in a sterilized container, and cover with a new brine. At the end of the curing time, the corned beef is ready to be eaten, canned, frozen, or simply left in the brine until needed or until it is no longer possible to keep the brine at a temperature of 34°F.

Dried beef is corned beef that has completed its cure, been removed from the brine, rinsed, and hung to dry off. It is then smoked to the desired consistency, wrapped loosely in paper, and hung in a cloth bag until dry. Dried beef is usually sliced very thin to use. If you don't wish to smoke the dried beef, hang it in an open, airy, insect-free place until completely dry before wrapping.

Corned beef can also be prepared in small batches in the refrigerator regardless of the weather. For approximately 10 pounds of meat, use the following ingredients, and prepare according to the directions for the larger quantities: 1 pound salt, 6 tablespoons sugar, and 1½ teaspoons baking soda. The meat should be ready to eat in about 3 weeks. Check the temperature in your refrigerator, and make sure the brine is kept at the proper temperature.

Poultry

Chickens, turkeys, ducks, geese, and capons can all be cured and smoked; however, the larger, fatter birds are best since the drying and smoking process greatly shrinks the birds. Any variety of domestic fowl may be mixed together and brined in the same crock. A variety of wild fowl can also be brined together; however, domestic and wild should be kept separated.

For 25 pounds of fowl, mix together 6½ pounds meat salt, 3½ pounds sugar, and 3 ounces saltpeter. Rub this mixture in dry for the dry sugar-cure. Dissolve in 4½ gallons of water to brine cure the fowl. Cure fowl for at least 1½ days per pound (15-pound turkey for 22½ days) or at least 2 weeks, but no more than 4 weeks.

Remove fowl from cure, rinse in fresh, cold water, and hang to dry. Birds are now ready to be smoked.

When brine-curing larger turkeys, remove the birds at least once a week, and stir the brine; then return the birds, changing their positions in the brine from top to bottom, bottom to top, etc. When dry-curing the larger turkeys, cure as hams, dividing the dry mixture in thirds and adding more mixture to the birds on the 3rd and 8th days. This is not necessary for smaller birds. Birds can also be split for easier curing and smoking.

Lamb

Lamb can be sugar cured or sweet-pickle cured in the same manner as ham. For 100 pounds of meat, use 8 pounds salt, 3 pounds brown or white sugar, and 2 ounces saltpeter. For the liquid cure, mix this with about 5 gallons of 35°F to 40°F water. Pack meat in a sterilized crock or barrel, and cover with brine. Keep brined meat at 35°F to 40°F, and cure at least 2 days per pound. Overhaul (switch meat around and stir up brine) on the 3rd and 5th days of curing. Again, watch the brine closely, and change if necessary.

To dry or sugar cure lamb, divide the dry cure into thirds, rubbing ⅓ of the mixture well into the meat. Apply the rest of the mixture on the 3rd and 5th days of curing. To dry cure requires only 1½ days per pound. Pack the meat in a crock or box, or lay on a shelf to cure.

At the end of the curing time, wash the meat well, and dry thoroughly. The meat can now be smoked if desired or simply wrapped in paper and hung in a cool, well-ventilated place. Meat must be kept dry, or mold will appear. If the meat starts to mold, wash off the mold with vinegar, or simply trim off the mold before using.

Wild Game

Antelope, bear, caribou, buffalo, deer, elk, and moose can all be dry or sweet-pickle cured. For 100 pounds of meat, use 10 pounds salt, 3 pounds sugar, and 2 ounces saltpeter. To dry cure the game, divide the mixture in thirds, rubbing one portion into the meat pieces. Pack the meat pieces into a sterilized crock or barrel, and keep at 35°F to 40°F. Resalt the meat on the 5th and 8th day. Two days per pound should be sufficient to cure the meat; however, the meat can be left in the cure until needed, or it can be cleaned and dried, wrapped in paper, and hung in a cool, well-ventilated place until needed.

To sweet-pickle cure, pack the meat into a sterilized crock or barrel. To the mixture, add 5 gallons of cool water and stir until dissolved. Pour this over the meat, weighting the meat to keep it under the brine, and keep in a cool, 35°F to 40°F place. Overhaul the meat on the 5th and 8th day of curing. Meat should cure 2½ to 3 days per pound, or it can be left in the curing mixture until needed. To dry the meat, remove it from the brine, wash and dry thoroughly, wrap in paper, and hang in a cool, well-ventilated place until needed.

Wild game can also be smoked before hanging if desired.

Small game such as squirrels, rabbits, woodchuck, raccoon, muskrats, etc., can be cured in a wet or dry cure using the same recipe for the larger game animals. The smaller animals can be processed whole or cut into serving pieces. Remember, the cut-up game will need only a small amount of time in the cure, unless you wish to leave them until used.

Quail, pheasant, ducks, geese, etc., should all be cured in the manner of domestic poultry.

Fish

Fish spoils more rapidly than other meats, and for that reason, special attention should be taken with the curing of fish. Clean the fish as soon as they are caught, and pack them in ice immediately. Fish will have to be kept cold at all times. Clean the fish however you desire: scale or skin, whole, sliced, or in fillets. If you wish to hang the fish for smoking, leave the collarbone in place. Fish that are processed whole should be spread open for curing and smoking. Fillets will have to be placed on racks to smoke. After cleaning fish, wash thoroughly and drain dry.

Fish can be preserved in several ways: either by starting with a dry cure and then thoroughly drying for storage, or brining and simply leaving the fish in the brine until needed, or by starting with one of the above methods and then smoking the fish before storage.

To dry cure fish, cover with salt, and pack the pieces in a wooden box with drainage holes in the bottom. Put a layer of salt in the bottom of the box, add a layer of salted fish, skin side down, sprinkle more salt over the fish, and add another layer of fish. Continue until all the fish are packed. You should use approximately a pound of salt for 4 pounds of fish.

The amount of time necessary for curing the fish is hard to determine. Because of the different varieties and size of fish, weather conditions, etc., it may take anywhere from a couple of days in warm weather to a week in cool weather.

After curing, remove from the box, scrub off all surface salt, and place on racks in the shade to dry. Keep turning the fish to insure that they dry thoroughly. Bring the fish in at night, and take back outside when the sun warms. You'll know when they are dried thoroughly because they will be firm and won't dent when squeezed between thumb and forefinger. They can be wrapped separately in waxed paper, placed in a tightly closed wooden box, and stored in a cool, dry place.

To brine cure fish, you will need about 1 pound salt to three pounds fish. Rub salt into the fish, and pack into a crock or wooden barrel with layers of salt between the layers of fish. Brine will form as the salt draws the moisture from the fish. Again, it will take anywhere from 2 days to a week to cure the fish. At the end of this time, the fish can be cleaned, dried, and smoked, or the fish can be cleaned and repacked into a brine solution for storage.

To store in a brine solution, clean the fish, and pack into a clean crock between layers of salt. Cover with a solution of 4 pounds salt dissolved in 1½ gallons of water. This should be stored in a cool place, and the brine should be watched carefully and changed as needed.

If you don't have a large volume of fish to cure, you might wish to make fish flakes. This can easily be done right in the kitchen, anytime of the year. Fillet fish; then bake in the oven until flaky. Spread drained flakes of fish onto parchment-lined cookie sheets, and dry in a 150°F oven. When dry, allow to cool, and pack into tightly closed containers.

SMOKING

Smoking is another of those ancient arts of food preservation, and it naturally fits in with curing meats to prolong the storage time. There is evidence that the stone-age people used smoking to help preserve meats for a time when hunting was bad. Smoking is also what gives cured meat its delicate and unusual flavoring. Who hasn't tasted a country cured and smoked ham and wished he could cure and smoke hams to taste like that? Or how about smoked fish or turkey, with its delicate aroma and flavoring that make it a gourmet special at any party? Smoking is actually quite easy and fun if you adhere to the safety rules and pay special attention to details. The old-time, hard-smoked meat often fed to sailors and armies is a far cry from the delicacies offered from today's smokers. Today home-smoking meats is big business and almost every magazine has advertisements selling small home smokers.

There are basically two types of smoking: cold smoking and hot smoking. Cold smoking uses a low, smoldering type of smoke. The temperature of the smoke house in cold smoking will seldom get above 100°F. This is the type of smoking normally used for hams, bacon, beef, or any meat that is to be preserved by curing and smoking. Hot smoking is actually a combination of smoking and cooking to prepare a meat for eating immediately. Naturally, if the meat is cooked as in hot smoking, it must be consumed at once or refrigerated for later use; it cannot simply be wrapped and hung up to store as can meats that have been cold smoked. In this book, we will discuss only cold smoking for storage.

There are so many variables in smoking that it is not really an exacting art. Each fish, fowl, or piece of meat may be somewhat different in moisture content, size, etc. So it's to your advantage to keep good records of what you smoked, how much it weighed, the amount of brining needed, and the proper amount of smoking for the end result. Then, only after experience, can you really predict to any degree the results of smoking different meats. Smoking does require some equipment, but it can be as simple or as complicated as you like. Primitive people merely use a cured animal skin draped over a framework of wooden branches or sticks and a small smoldering smoky fire. One of the simplest methods and perhaps the best if you merely want to try your hand at smoking, is to purchase one of the popular commercial smokers. These, however, are made to hold only small portions of meat and won't suffice if you plan on smoking larger pieces of meat.

Another simple smoker consists of a cleaned, wooden 50-gallon barrel or metal drum. Both ends must be cut out of the barrel or drum.

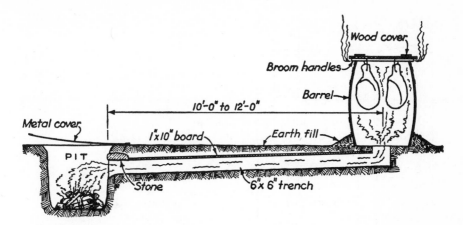

Barrel smoker.

The idea in smoking is not to cook the meat but to allow the smoke to dry and flavor the meat, so the fire shouldn't be built in the container holding the meat. Instead, dig a hole in the ground as shown above. This hole is the fire pit. Run a stove pipe or tile in a trench from the top of the fire pit to the bottom of the barrel as shown. This trench must run uphill to the barrel so the smoke will travel up to the barrel-smoke-house properly. Place a metal cover over the fire pit so you can control the amount of air taken into it and as a result the heat and amount of flame in the fire. Place a couple of broom handles or sturdy limbs across the top of the barrel, and hang the meat from these. Make a wooden top to place over the broom handles. If you wish more control over the amount of smoke escaping from the barrel, place a heavy tarp or cloth over the barrel top. Another thing you can do to improve this type of barrel-smokehouse is to make a baffle that will fit over the smoke hole in the bottom of the barrel. This is simply a wooden or metal plate with a number of holes cut in it. This forces the smoke to spread out as it rises in the barrel, rather than going up in one straight column.

Although this type of smokehouse is large enough for the average use, another type of smokehouse that is a bit larger can be made by utilizing an old refrigerator. Remove the bottom, and cut a hole in the top for ventilation as shown in the illustration on page 218. Again, the smoke pit should be placed some distance from the smokehouse to insure that the smoke is "cold" smoke.

If you use an old refrigerator, make sure you remove the old latch, place an ordinary padlock on it, and keep it padlocked shut when not in use so children won't get in it and play.

You can also make a permanent smokehouse if you wish, and

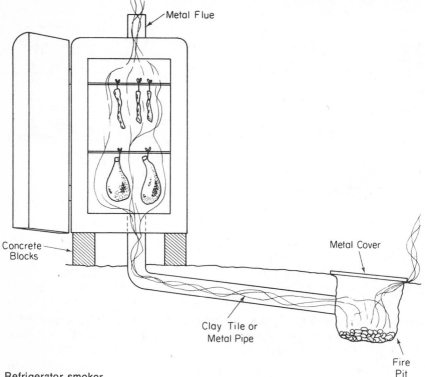

Refrigerator smoker.

use it not only for smoking but for storing meats after you have finished smoking them.

The main thing is to make sure the smokehouse, fire pit, and all portions of the smoking apparatus are tightly constructed and fitted with good ventilators so you can utilize every bit of smoke.

Smoking Pork

Regardless of what type of meat is to be smoked, it should first be prepared by curing in a brine solution, either dry or sweet-pickle brine. After curing, remove from the packing barrel, and brush off surface cure. If cured in brine, soak meat in cold, fresh water for about a half hour to soak off some of the surface salt. Use heavy duty string to make loops for hanging meat in the smokehouse. Hams and shoulders should be tied through the shank. Light pieces such as bacon should be reinforced with wooden skewers. After stringing, scrub the meat clean with hot

Before hanging cured meat in smoker, scrub clean to remove all dry cure or brine from the surface of the meat.

water and a sharp brush. (See above illustration.) The water should be about 110°F to 125°F. Then hang up, and allow to dry. If you don't get the meat scrubbed clean and allow it to dry thoroughly, the smoke won't take well, and the meat will be streaked in appearance. The meat should hang overnight in a cool place.

Carefully hang the meat in the smokehouse so that none of the pieces are touching. Build a fire of some kind of hardwood, oak, apple, hickory, or even corn cobs, in the fire pit. Above all, don't build the fire of softwood such as pine. Pine smoke is sooty and filled with pitch, which will flavor the meat strongly. Place a thermometer in the smokehouse, and allow the smokehouse to heat up to about 100°F or 120°F, or just hot enough to melt the surface fat on the pork. Then open the top ventilator just a bit to let out any moisture. On the second day, close the ventilator, and continue to smoke for at least one more day, or until the meat takes on the desired color.

You don't have to have a dense cloud of smoke—a slight haze will work just as well. The main thing is not to overheat the meat after the first day and scorch or cook it; remember you're *cold smoking* the meat.

The best kind of fire is one built in the Indian fashion of sticks radiating out from the center like a wheel. As the sticks burn, you can continue to push the sticks into the center and add more wood. This type of fire will become cooler and lower rather than hotter as it burns. One of the main problems with smoking is inattention to the fire and

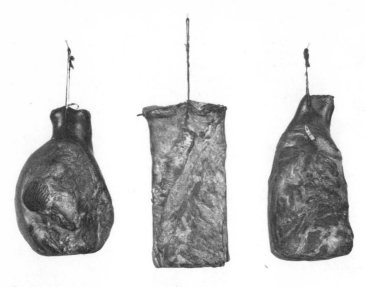

Smoked ham, bacon, and shoulder.

the resulting ruined meat in the smokehouse. You can also use twigs or green sawdust to dampen a fire and make it smoke better. The warm smoked meat should be tested with a ham trier or a clean, stiff wire run into the meat. It should be run in along the bone to the center of the ham and then withdrawn. If it has a sour odor, the meat is tainted. If it doesn't have a sour odor, or if it smells sweet, the meat is sound. If you get a tainted odor, cut open the meat, and examine for spoilage. If the meat gives off a definite odor of putrefaction, you'll have to destroy the entire piece of meat.

After the meat has been smoked to your satisfaction, it should be wrapped and bagged for storage. If the meat isn't properly wrapped, it will become infested with insects. Common insects that cause problems are the larder beetle, mites, skipper flies, and the red-legged ham beetle. You should plan your curing and smoking processes so the meat will be safely bagged before warm spring weather arrives. The first step is to wrap the meat in heavy paper as shown on page 221. Some people also like to rub on a bit of black and a little bit of red pepper before wrapping. After wrapping in paper, place in a muslin bag, and hang in a safe, cool, dark, dry place that is well ventilated. If properly cured, smoked, and stored, hams will often keep a year or longer and will develop a mellow flavor that is characteristic of country-cured pork. The string hanging the meat should be tied to the bags and not the meat, or insects may find their way into the meat through the strings.

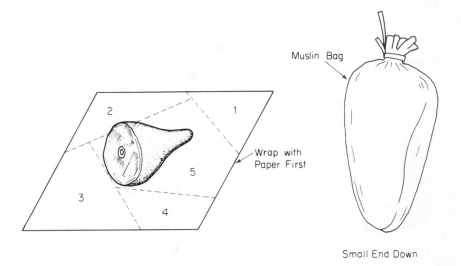

Muslin Bag

Wrap with
Paper First

Small End Down

Wrapping ham.

Some people like to protect the meat further by painting the bag with a protective coating called a *yellow wash*. The solution is made of 3 pounds barium sulfate, 1¼ ounces yellow ocher, 1 ounce dry glue, 6 ounces flour, and a pail half full of water. Mix the flour in the water to make sure there are no lumps; then mix the coloring agent in a quart of water, pour in the glue, and then pour this into the flour and water mixture. Slowly bring to a boil; then slowly add the barium sulfate, stirring constantly. It's a good idea to make up this mixture the day before it is to be used, and keep it stirred up. When ready to use, paint it on the bags with a clean paint brush.

Even with the best of storage processes, you will end up with a bit of surface mold on the hams and shoulders. This can easily be trimmed off before use. Smaller pieces such as bacon are best placed in the freezer or used quite quickly as they don't keep as well as the larger pieces.

Smoking Beef

Cured beef may be smoked in much the same manner as pork, and it not only aids in the preservation but gives it a more desirable flavor and appearance, as well as drying it out better. It should be stored in a cool, dark, dry, well-ventilated place.

Smoking Lamb

Smoke for a couple of days at temperatures of 100°F to 120°F. Make sure that the grease doesn't drip and run into the fire pit, causing a flare up.

Smoking Poultry and Fowl

Both wild fowl and poultry may be smoked. Make sure the temperature in the smokehouse doesn't go over 90°F, or it will start to cook the bird. Poultry is properly smoked when it reaches a deep, dark mahogany color.

Game Animals

Game animals can be smoked the same as pork, beef, and lamb.

Fish

When the brine time is up, remove the fish, drain, and rinse off all surface salt. The fish should be dried thoroughly before smoking in order to form the "pellicle," a thin, glossy sheen that helps the fish take the smoke better. Drying time may take as much as 2 or 3 hours before this forms on the surface of the fish, but it is necessary. This thin film helps hold in the juices during the smoking process. After the pellicle is formed, the fish is ready to be smoked.

Don't allow the temperature in the smokehouse to get above 70°F, and place the fish on wire racks coated with cooking oil, or hang the fish up by the collarbone using small S-shaped hooks. If you plan on keeping the fish only a couple of weeks, you can smoke them for about 24 hours, but the longer they are smoked, the longer they will keep. This will take a bit of experimentation. Fish is quite perishable, and once you start the smoking process, it should be continued until you intend to quit. After smoking, remove the fish, allow it to cool, and package for storage by wrapping in paper and then cloth bags. It should then be placed in an airtight container.

DRYING

Like drying fruits and vegetables, drying meats is probably one of the oldest methods of preserving food for later consumption. Drying is also one of the simplest methods. You can dry almost any kind of meat, but it must be lean, and you must cut off all fat. Any fat that is left on will not only hamper the drying process but will become rancid when the meat is stored.

Incidentally, red meats cannot be properly dried in the sun. You will need the use of an oven or a homemade or commercial dryer to properly dry any of the red meats.

Although many dried meats such as jerky or pemmican are meant to be eaten without cooking, thinly sliced dried beef and wild game as well as dried fowl and fish can be used as the basis of many soups, stews, and chowders. There are many recipes created exclusively for dried meats, and in these recipes, the dried meat is used as is. However, the meat can be reconstituted by soaking overnight ½ cup meat to 2 cups water. It can then be used in many recipes calling for fresh meat. The reconstituted meat is usually too salty and tough to be fried.

Jerky

Jerky is one of my favorite foods, and I always carry a small bag of it when I'm hiking or hunting. It's not only pleasant and tasty to chew on but nourishing as well, and it sure beats carrying candy or other junk. Jerky was made by the American Indians, who used venison, elk, and buffalo. You can make it out of almost any lean, red meat including beef. However, to my taste, it is best when made out of venison, probably because venison has almost no marbling of fat in it. If you make jerky from venison, pork, or bear, make sure you first freeze the meat at 0°F to kill trichinae, which is a parasite that can give you trichinosis if these meats are not properly frozen or thoroughly cooked.

The first step in preparing the meat is to slice it *with the grain*

To make jerky, slice lean cuts of meat in thin strips with the grain.

into very thin strips. It will slice better if it is chilled overnight in the coldest part of your refrigerator. After slicing, cut off all fat.

The flavoring of jerky is provided by the juices it is marinated in, and there are literally hundreds of recipes for jerky. Following is my favorite recipe. You may wish to add additional seasonings to suit your taste.

Place strips in a shallow pan; then pour in enough water to cover the meat well. Shake in about a tablespoon of Worchestershire sauce, a couple drops of Tabasco sauce, then add 1 tablespoon salt, ½ teaspoon black pepper, 2 tablespoons powdered onion, and 1 teaspoon garlic powder. Marinate the meat overnight in the refrigerator.

Remove, drain strips on paper toweling, and place on the racks in your oven. Place a drip pan underneath to catch any juice that may run out. Turn oven to lowest setting, and leave door open slightly. Dry until jerky is black and like leather. When bent, it should crack but not break. It normally takes about 2 to 3 hours to properly dry jerky.

When dry, place it in a dark, tightly sealed container. I like to place a handful of jerky strips in several small plastic food bags, tie them shut, and place them in a metal tin. When I want a snack to take with me to the woods, I merely grab a bag of jerky.

Dried jerky should be tough and leathery, but should not break when bent.

Pemmican

If you like jerky, you'll probably like another Indian food—pemmican. It is made in much the same manner as jerky; however, if you are going to make pemmican, it is best to slice the meat *across the grain*. After marinating and drying the meat, pound or grind it into very fine pieces. Add an equal amount of ground or chopped raisins, dried berries, apricots, and peaches and an equal amount of nuts such as peanuts or pecans. Add a dash of ground red pepper, and moisten with honey and peanut butter. Mix together thoroughly; then place in small plastic bags, and tie shut. If kept in a cool, dry place, pemmican will last for years. Not only is it an excellent snack for hunters and hikers on the trail, but by adding a bit of water and flour and simmering it, you can make an excellent camp stew.

Easy Dried Meat

This recipe can be used for almost any meat: pork, beef, lamb, wild game, poultry, and wild fowl. The meat should be roasted in a slow (300°F to 325°F) oven until tender. Keep a cover on the roaster to prevent the meat from crusting over while cooking. When done, drain, place in the refrigerator, and chill overnight. (Broth can be canned or frozen and used later with meat recipes.) The next day, use a very sharp knife or meat slicer to slice the meat as thin as possible *with the grain*. If you cut against the grain, the meat will crumble into tiny pieces. Make sure the meat is thoroughly chilled so you can easily cut it thin.

Spread the meat slices out on racks in your oven (with a drip pan underneath) or on parchment paper on cookie sheets. The oven should be set at warm, or about 150°F, with the door left open slightly. If your oven is gas heated, make sure that the flame doesn't go out and asphyxiate everyone. The meat is done when it is almost black and will bend and crack but not break when twisted. After drying meat strips, place in a tightly covered container such as a metal lard can or similar storage container, and store in a cool, dark, dry place.

MISCELLANEOUS MEAT RECIPES

Pastrami

This delicacy is nothing more than corned beef with herbs added to the brine. Juniper berries and other spices have traditionally been used to impart the unusual flavor; you will need to experiment to find the right amounts and kinds of herbs you like best. The main thing is to add a bit of chopped garlic cloves to the brine solution.

The best meats to use for pastrami are beef briskets, and they should be cured in the brine solution for two weeks at 34°F to 40°F. Remove, and hang up to dry in a cool, dry place with plenty of ventilation. After hanging for about a day, smoke the pastrami in a smokehouse. Place a thermometer so that it reads the center of the cured beef briskets, and smoke with a low fire until the thermometer reaches 140°F. Remove, wrap, and store as for corned beef.

Mincemeat

Mincemeat is one of those old-time favorites that is not only good to eat but also very practical. Mincemeat was a favorite food with the old-timers because it was one way of stretching a meager meat supply, and today that can be just as important. Mincemeat pie is also one of those childhood delights that you just can't forget. My favorite kind of mincemeat is made from venison, but you can use almost any meat scraps, even cooked beef roast or small pieces of steak.

The first steps in making mincemeat if you are using uncooked meats are to place bony pieces of meat in a pan, cover with water, and boil until the meat falls from the bones. Drain meat, and remove it from bones and fat; then grind meat in a home food-grinder. You will need between 6 and 8 cups of meat.

Grind peeled and cored apples to make 8 cups of ground apples.

Remove seeds and core from 3 lemons and 6 oranges, and grind. In a large kettle, mix together meat, apples, oranges, and lemons, and add the following:

> 3 cups white sugar
> 3 cups brown sugar
> 6 pounds raisins, light and dark
> 1 tablespoon salt
> 1 tablespoon cinnamon
> 1 tablespoon nutmeg
> 2 teaspoons ginger
> 2 teaspoons cloves
> 1 teaspoon allspice

Mix all ingredients together thoroughly, and bring to a boil. Cook for 10 minutes, adding strained meat broth if needed for more liquid.

Pack hot into pint jars, and process in pressure canner for 60 minutes at 10 pounds pressure.

You can also make up pie shells, pour the mincemeat into these, and freeze them for later use.

Because mincemeat pie flavoring is a personal thing, you can also add anything you wish in the way of fruits, etc. Some people like to add bits of candied fruits, orange juice or sweet cider, dates, nuts, currants, figs, and even a bit of brandy.

Summer Sausage

This hard, dry, highly seasoned sausage is a favorite with gourmet food lovers, and one you will have a lot of fun experimenting with. If properly made and stored in a dry place where it won't start to mold, it can be kept a long time. In fact, longer storage will often result in a delightful blending of flavors and an improvement in taste. Eventually mold will form on the casing, but this can be removed by rubbing the casing with a cloth dipped in vinegar. It can be served without being cooked and is excellent on crackers with cheese and a bit of wine. It does take a bit of time to make, and you shouldn't hurry any of the curing processes.

The first step is to cut up about 5 pounds of lean pork into small, bite-sized pieces. Spread these out on waxed paper in a single layer, and place in your deep freeze. Store for about a week at 0°F. Then remove the frozen pork from the freezer, and let thaw. Cut about 10 pounds lean beef into tiny pieces. Remove all the fat you can, because fat causes the sausage to become rancid-tasting.

Grind the meats together using a plate with $3/16$ inch holes, and mix in the following seasonings:

½ pound salt
1 tablespoon saltpeter
2 tablespoons black pepper, ground
2 tablespoons sage
2 tablespoons sugar
1½ teaspoons white pepper
Ground garlic

After mixing the meats and spices, regrind using a plate with ⅛ inch holes, grinding until all meat is very fine. Spread mixture in a large flat pan and store in your refrigerator for a couple of days. Make muslin casings by cutting cloth into 8 x 20 inch rectangles and by sewing along sides and 1 end. Place casings in water to soak; then stuff sausage into casings, tying off each casing with a string. Rub the outside of the casings with a sugar cure mix, and place in the refrigerator for a couple of days.

For better flavor, the sausages should be smoked in a very cool smokehouse (85°F to 90°F) for about 14 hours or until the muslin cases turn a deep, dark brown. Hang up to store in a cool, dry place. You can keep summer sausage in your refrigerator if you prefer.

Burch Family Hams

This recipe will make enough mix to cure 1 large ham.

> 1 pint meat salt
> 3 tablespoons brown sugar
> 2 tablespoons black pepper, ground
> 1 tablespoon red pepper, ground

Mix the ingredients together well using your hands. Spread a large sheet of clean, brown paper or several sheets of newspaper out on a table. Spread a layer of the mix in the middle of the paper, and place ham skin-side down on the mix. Rub the rest of the mix well into the ham, making sure you get the mix rubbed in around the bones. Wrap the paper around the ham, being careful not to knock off the mix. Wrap the ham tightly, but do not tape or tie. Hold the paper in place, and slide the ham into a muslin bag. Fold and pin the bag so that it holds the ham, cure, and paper tightly in place. Tie a knot in the end of the muslin bag, and tie a rope to this to hang the ham. The ham is simply hung up and left. If not eaten by warm weather, it can be taken down, wiped off, and placed in the freezer until needed, or it can be smoked in the spring and rehung throughout the summer.

Pork Sausage

Here is the recipe for sausage that we always use:

> 20 pounds pork trimmings, not too fat
> ½ cup meat salt
> ¼ cup black pepper
> 1 tablespoon red pepper or 1 tablespoon ground pod-pepper plus
>   1 teaspoon ground red pepper

Spread the meat trimmings out on a table, and sprinkle the seasonings over the meat. Mix together with your hands; then grind through a plate with 1/8 inch holes.

Stuff into muslin casings, or make into patties, and freeze with waxed paper between each patty.

Sage, ginger, cloves, nutmeg, and sugar are quite often added to sausage; you might wish to add one or all to the above recipe.

To smoke sausage, stuff into muslin casings, and let cure in a cool spot for 24 hours. Smoke at a temperature of 70°F to 90°F until the casings are a dark mahogany color. This sausage cannot be hung and kept in warm weather. It will have to be frozen or canned if kept through the summer.

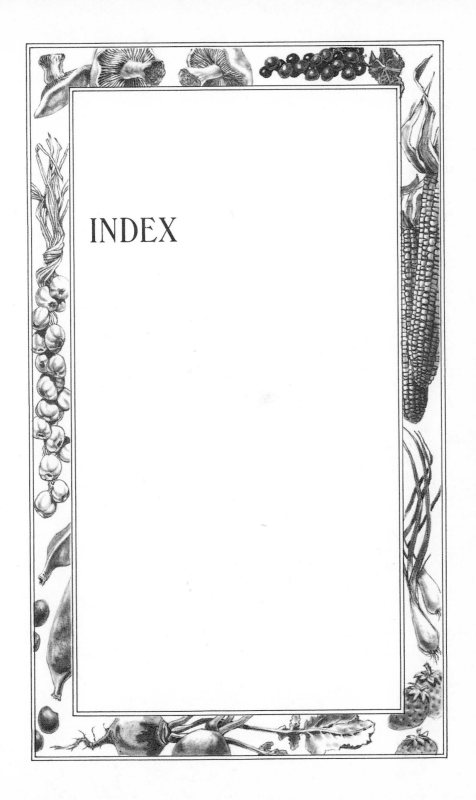

INDEX